THE GUIDE TO STRATEGIC NETWORKING

THE GUIDE TO STRATEGIC NETWORKING

DREAM. PLAN. CREATE. ACHIEVE.

Juliette C. Mayers

ISBN-10: 1470146452
ISBN-13: 9781470146450
Library of Congress Control Number: 2015914890
CreateSpace Independent Publishing Platform
North Charleston, South Carolina

To Darryl—Love Always

CONTENTS

Praise for

The Guide To Strategic Networking
Dream. Plan. Create. Achieve.

Inspirational and practical are two words that describe this masterpiece.
—J. Keith Motley PhD, Chancellor, University of Massachusetts Boston

Juliette Mayers is an inspirational leader with a passion for helping others succeed. In this book she provides specific action steps to illuminate the path to career and business success.
—Claire Muhm, President, The Boston Club

The Guide to Strategic Networking is the professional networking book you've been waiting for. It is packed with hands-on information that will help you take action. I highly recommend this book for growing your business.
—Bob Rivers, President, Eastern Bank

Juliette Mayers started her career as a management trainee at GE Capital and literally networked her way up the ladder and through the corridors of some of America's largest corporations and institutions to launch her own company, Inspiration Zone. Juliette offers readers practical, actionable advice that even a first time networker can use to advance his or her career. This book is a must-read for those serious about learning how to network strategically.
—Colette Phillips, CEO, CPC Global and Founder of Get Konnected

The Guide to Strategic Networking exemplifies that when passion meets planning and inspiration, great things happen.
—Yvonne Garcia, National Chairwoman of ALPFA and
SVP, Investment Manager Services, State Street Corporation

The most successful individuals and businesses understand the power of networking. This book represents an outstanding roadmap because Juliette Mayers is truly a networking guru.
—Phil Johnston, President and CEO, Johnston Associates

This is an important how-to-book, and Juliette Mayers is the perfect seasoned executive to share her perspective about the value of networking to advance your career.
—Marian L. Heard, President and CEO, Oxen Hill Partners, Retired President and CEO, The United Way of Massachusetts Bay and CEO of the United Ways of New England

If you're ready to take your business to the next level, this is a "must-read" book.
—Paul Guzzi, Chairman, Citi Center for The Performing Arts

One of the key ingredients to managing a successful career is our ability to build strong lasting relationships and to master the art of networking. Finding our own formula to do so effectively is an individual journey yet there are proven strategies and best practices to draw upon. Juliette's book provides practical advice and techniques that provide us with an effective roadmap.
—Rita Balian Allen, President of Rita B. Allen Associates and Author of Personal Branding and Marketing Yourself

INTRODUCTION

The biggest adventure you can ever take
is to live the life of your dreams.
—OPRAH WINFREY

I t's one thing to seek advice. Taking action, however, involves a different level of commitment. My goal in writing this book is to inspire you to achieve your dreams through the creation and activation of your own strategic networking action plan.

Too often, dreams go unfulfilled without plans. Yes, there are those who are born into powerful, well-connected families and seem to have life rigged in their favor. This book is for everyone else. An essential part of attaining one's dreams is the active support and engagement of other people. As the saying goes, "it takes a village." What is often not understood is how to develop and manage that village. Also, today's concept of "village" reaches beyond the physical to the digital and social connections that make up our modern-day network.

This book draws upon many of the same principles as my first book, *A Black Woman's Guide to Networking,* which had received all five-star reviews by Amazon.com members as of August 2015. Read the reviews, and you will notice that the book's appeal reached beyond the primary target audience—black women. The online feedback was consistent with verbal feedback from fans of the book who wanted to make the content more accessible to all audiences. I recall one of my book signings, where a small group of men waited for the crowd to thin out before approaching me to purchase the book. One man spoke for the group. They were colleagues who had heard great things about the book but didn't feel comfortable standing in the all-women line given the title of the book. As I was writing to fill a void in the marketplace, I have no apologies for the title of my first book, but I did learn a lot from talking to people of all backgrounds and races—men and women alike. What I learned is that a hunger exists in the marketplace for simplicity, accessibility, and cross-cultural learning—now more so than ever before.

While some challenges and nuances are unique to diverse, multicultural professionals, most of the issues related to professional networking resonate with broader audiences. Many experience a deeply rooted fear of reaching out beyond their personal comfort zones. I define comfort zone as that which makes one feel safe—it is the opposite of risk taking. Inherent in the process of relationship building and networking is the risk of rejection, the possibility of failure, and for those whose energy comes from within, the energy drain that can follow networking events.

Even for people who enjoy social gatherings and professionally connecting with others, the question "Toward what end?" often lingers. In one case, a middle-aged white male shared the fact that he was pretty well networked but that he still felt stuck. He saw a lot of the same people at the events he attended and felt a sense of comfort with that. He had developed what he described as "pretty good relationships." What he did not have, despite frequent attendance at networking events, was a clear vision or a plan for effectively advancing his business agenda. His story is a common one.

With this book, I aim to increase the circle. *The Guide to Strategic Networking* builds upon the framework and principles discussed in my first book and incorporates excerpts from it, including selected Networking

Masters. The content has been expanded and updated, with a greater focus on action planning. The inspirational stories sprinkled throughout the book, however, have not changed.

Many books on the topic of networking are available. At its core, effective networking is about relationships and practices that allow you to attain your measure of success. What is unique about this book is its atypical approach, its appreciation of the challenges of diverse professions, and its practical implementation tools. Its ultimate goal is to guide you toward the attainment of your dream.

My hope is that this book will inspire you to do the following:

Dream. Create your personal vision—your "grand vision" of what you would like to achieve.
Plan. Construct a roadmap—goals and tactics in support of your vision.
Create. Develop and effectively manage your network.
Achieve. Attain your personal, professional, and business goals.

A networking book would not be complete without addressing the role of digital and social media. Given the popularity of Facebook, Twitter, LinkedIn, Instagram, personal websites, and blogs, not surprisingly, professionals are struggling to find balance. I will explore how these tools can enable your networking strategy when used selectively.

Whether you are trying to advance your career, start or grow your business, or increase your personal effectiveness, you are the single biggest influence on your success. Yes, barriers and roadblocks are challenges that you must overcome in order to attain your goal. Sadly, societal "isms" are still alive—sexism, ageism, and racism are very real and thriving in many organizations and in our communities. It is important to be educated and conscious of our own biases and those of others, as they have the potential to derail your plans. More importantly, your mind-set must acknowledge that "anything is possible"—a mental toughness and a passion about your dream will fuel your perseverance and persistence. The intent is not to ignore your challenges or to minimize them but to focus on the common success factors and the relationships that are needed to achieve your dream.

What is the common thread linking those who reach the pinnacle of success? They never let go of their dreams. They believe deeply in themselves and in their purpose—so much so that they are *passionate* about their work. They put in the time and effort to learn continuously, and they acquire expertise by practicing their craft. They develop and nurture others and give generously, and when times get tough, they draw on the strength of their relationships.

This book has been created in a format that allows you to develop a Strategic Networking Action Plan. Research has shown that written plans have a much higher likelihood of being implemented.

Action exercises entitled "Making It Real" appear at key intervals—these are designed to help you maximize your learning and serve as inputs for your plan. So that you can get the most from this book, I highly recommend that you complete these exercises. I suggest that you read through the book first and then reread it as you practice various aspects of your networking strategy. Once you're conscious of your actions and have ensured they align with your plan, you should strive to develop a mastery of them. You'll know when you have done so, because you will have reached a point where you no longer focus on the tactics of your plan—these will become intuitive.

I wish you success on your strategic networking journey. I am honored to be your guide. I welcome your stories and experiences. You can reach me at juliette@juliettemayers.com and follow me on Twitter @jcmayers.

PART I: DREAM

CHAPTER 1

DREAM IMAGINED

A dream doesn't become reality through magic;
it takes sweat, determination and hard work.
—COLIN POWELL

I magine you're a ten-year-old child on your way to a new country without your parents. It's your first time on an airplane, and you're going to live with your grandmother, whom you have not seen in five years. Your last memory of your grandmother is an image of her making coconut bread. You watch as she grates the coconut on a shiny object. The flakes are fluffy. They are brown and white and smell really good. The aroma is wonderful. When your grandmother (Gran-Gran) speaks about America, she talks in a very heavy accent. It's one that you know well. It is stronger than your mother's. She speaks about a land of opportunity and a place to where she longs to return in order to build a better life for her family. Her plan is to send for her children and her grandchildren over time. The plane ride reminds you of her. Going through the puffy white clouds is exciting. It feels like a dream, but it's real. The flight attendant is wearing a dark blue uniform. She is very nice. She is pretty. She reminds you of one of your teachers. She gives you two shiny silver bags of peanuts and a plastic object with red, white, and blue colors. It's a small airplane. You like it. As you hold the small plastic plane, you realize that you are on your way to the place you've heard so much about. It's the place you have dreamed about. It's the land of opportunity—it's America!

As an entrepreneur, author, and professional speaker, I am the "poster child" for the power of networking. I share the journey of many immigrants and have benefited from the principles that I now share with you in this book. I learned very early on the importance of having big dreams. My mom, who came to the United States one year after my arrival, inspired me in my educational pursuits and in passionately chasing the American dream. While she did not have a formal education, she knew that education could break the chains of poverty. She was a woman with a clear vision for her children. She articulated her dream and, more importantly, executed on her plan.

CHAPTER 2

STRATEGIC NETWORKING DEFINED

For many professionals, business planning is an annual event. It usually starts with direction from the business owner or chief executive who articulates the vision. Goals are established along with specific initiatives for how the goals will be accomplished and measured. This process is then communicated at every level of the organization in terms that are relevant to the particular worker or employee. Budgets and human resource allocation are also important considerations for execution of the plan. For some organizations, the process is very formal; others may have a more relaxed approach. The point is that most well-run organizations have a strategic planning process. While many professionals engage in such a process on behalf of their employers, too often they have no plan for executing the hopes and dreams they hold dearest—their own.

Strategic networking is the art of networking in ways that are aligned with your vision and strategy. Implicit in this concept is the idea that you will network with a purpose in mind. As such, strategic networking means that you must align your resources, time, energy, and mindfulness to the things that matter and that are aligned with the attainment of your dreams. It requires the creation and management of your personal action plan in ways that will maximize your effectiveness and support your goals. When you are operating strategically, it is counterproductive to wander aimlessly at events or forums that have no relevance to your work or longer-term plan. It requires focus and the ability to say no to activities that consume your time without any benefit to you and that are not in alignment with your objectives. This does not mean you should be self-centered and/or deprioritize friends, family, and colleagues. In fact, I strongly encourage you to develop an integrated action plan. The people you hold dear should be front and center and must be considered in your overall visioning and planning.

Too often, networking is thought of only at major life transitions—entry into the workforce, loss of a job, desire to land a board seat, and start-up or expansion of a business. Such major transitions naturally require support from others, and the people most likely to secure that support are those who have cultivated relationships and are prepared for the opportunity they seek. They are often viewed as "lucky," but they are the ones who likely created a strategic network before they needed it.

The good news is that it is never too late to build your networking skill set. Regardless of where you are on your journey, I strongly encourage you to make it a focus. Most likely you know someone, or know of someone, who lost a job. The stories of people who worked at corporations for many years and then suddenly became unemployed are heart wrenching—and the story is worse when such individuals neglected to build a professional network beyond the walls of their employers. The reasons they didn't do so are all legitimate—demanding job, impossible hours, no time to grab lunch much less engage externally, and a feeling of job security. In today's workaday world, why professionals may see networking as a chore, yet another task to add to the brimming pile of "to-dos," is easy to understand.

First, I acknowledge the difficulty in managing the demands of a corporate job. I lived in corporate America for twenty-nine years with some of the best-run companies in the world. Now, as the CEO of my own firm, Inspiration Zone LLC, I too have a lot of demands on my time. The number of hours in a day is the same for all of us, so it comes down to managing energy and time, which means we must master prioritization. Having a plan will help you feel more energized, because it will give you clarity of goals and purpose. Strategic networking will lead to mutually rewarding relationships and will help to position you well for life's transitions. The peace of mind and positive energy that comes from having a strong and vibrant network will enrich your life in many ways.

Strategic networking can be time-consuming if you treat it as a separate function. I suggest that you use an integrated approach, meaning that you should look for ways to *enhance what you are already doing*. I also strongly recommend a comprehensive approach that takes into account your personal life. Too often, personal commitments and family well-being are left out of the mix, which can lead to stress as you struggle to achieve the elusive balance. Your opportunities for integration will become clearer once you've created or updated your action plan.

In order to increase your effectiveness, you must create or tap into networks that are both strategic and productive. Ultimately you want to spend your time on those activities that will get you closer to your goals as you simultaneously develop and sustain relationships that are mutually beneficial.

Goals are an important component of your plan. In the sections ahead, we will talk more about goals and how they can help you prioritize and align your activities.

Making It Real Action Exercise:
Identifying My Networking Interests

The topic of strategic networking is intriguing to me because I want to do the following: (check all that apply)

- Find a job or position myself for my next opportunity.
- Start a new venture or business.
- Grow or expand my existing business.
- Accelerate career growth within my corporation/organization.
- Prepare for my retirement.
- Broaden or strengthen my already robust network.
- Diversify my network by ethnicity and culture.
- Enrich my development by meeting interesting people.
- Get to know more professionals in my field.
- Effectively manage my extensive network of contacts.
- Attract a powerful mentor and/or sponsor.
- Share my expertise and knowledge
- Land a seat on a community or corporate board
- Other(s)_____

CHAPTER 3

YOUR GRAND VISION

D ream big! Why not? As adults, we have been conditioned to self-edit our dreams. The practice of self-editing often leads us to scale back our big hopes and aspirations for our professional and personal visions. In fact, thinking of reasons why *not* to pursue our grand visions is often easier than thinking of reasons why we should. Risks, costs, and political land mines lie in wait for big thinkers. There is always a price to be paid—the sacrifice of time, hard work, and perseverance; the vulnerability that comes with working outside one's comfort zone; and of course, the price of failure. But contrast those perceived negatives with the rewards—passion, fulfilling and gratifying work, continuous learning, enhanced self-esteem, boundless energy, excitement, and the satisfaction of making a memorable difference in the world.

You may not have given yourself permission to create a grand vision—or at least not one that you would share publicly. As an author, I have met lots of people who shared their vision to be a published author and to influence the world through thought leadership. Some people have completed multiple manuscripts and yet have talked themselves out of taking the subsequent steps toward publication. Others have allowed naysayers and dream snatchers to rob them of their precious gems. A few were inspired to persevere and fulfill their dream—they are now published authors.

Here is one of my favorite quotes by Marianne Williamson.

Our deepest fear is not that we are inadequate. Our deepest fear is that we are powerful beyond measure. It is our light, not our darkness, that most frightens us. We ask ourselves, who am I to be brilliant, gorgeous, talented, and fabulous? Actually, who are you not to be? You are a child of God. Your playing small doesn't serve the world. There's nothing enlightened about shrinking so that other people won't feel insecure around you. We are all meant to shine, as children do. We are born to make manifest the glory of God that is within us. It's not just in some of us; it's in everyone. And as we let our own light shine, we unconsciously give other people permission to do the same. As we are liberated from our own fear, our presence automatically liberates others. (Marianne Williamson)

When it comes to having a vision, I often tell people to dream what's possible. Have a vision. This is another way of saying "know where you want to go." Yes, there are those who may have stumbled through life and have achieved a measure of success. You can't assume that you will be the lucky one. Your vision should be bold. Don't hold back. Too often we place constraints on what is possible because we confine our dreams to the physical and emotional space that others provide for us. We don't want others to be uncomfortable. We want to fit in at all costs. We place artificial limits on ourselves based on what we see around us and on the experiences of other people within our sphere of reference.

In order to have a breakthrough experience, we must unleash the mental process that allows us to think big. Don't allow your current circumstances to define your possibilities. Look beyond your own experiences and your own networks for inspiration. Craft a new vision for yourself.

I want to underscore the importance of taking this step. You may be a highly accomplished corporate executive; if so, at some time in your career, you will have completed an exercise or process that included developing a vision statement. You may have helped or coached others in the development of their vision statements—but have you done yours lately? If you have, go ahead and complete the exercise. It should be a breeze for you.

For those who have not completed a personal vision statement or those in need of a refresher, your vision statement should be the expression of what you wish to achieve in the future, usually five to ten years out, although I recommend five years.

My personal vision statement is to help others achieve their dreams. I have outlined a plan by which I can fulfill my vision, including the writing of this book and the creation of my company, Inspiration Zone LLC, in 2011. Much has been written about vision statements. The prevailing wisdom is that good vision statements are concise, easy to commit to memory, and inspiring of action. If your vision is difficult for you to remember, it is likely too complicated. Strive for simplicity. Making the complex simple is generally more difficult, because you must filter through all of the extraneous information and make a decision on where to focus.

Your vision statement should reflect your values—the set of principles by which you lead your life. It doesn't necessarily need to include those exact words, though. To achieve strong momentum and to be passionate about your vision, it should be congruent with your beliefs and values.

Making It Real Action Exercise:
Developing My Grand Vision

Fast forward to the year 2020. I have achieved my dream, as evidenced by the attention of the news media and trade publications. (Choose the national media outlet that breaks the story of your significant accomplishment. Select your top three, or write in others)

- New York Times
- Fortune Magazine
- CNN
- Univision
- Fox News
- The Wall Street Journal
- Black Enterprise
- Center for Asian-American Media
- Entrepreneur Magazine
- Huffington Post
- Other(s): _____

(Imagine the fulfillment of your grand vision and write the headline for the press release.) For example, "Cyndra X. Johnson named CEO of XYZ Corporation, a $10 billion…"

My headline for my press release is:

_____

_____

_____

(If this is the first time you're doing this type of exercise for yourself, you can start smaller by substituting a local publication or media, but I encourage you not to skip this exercise. It will help you to think of those big dreams that you have deferred and to create a point of focus for your networking activities.)

Continuing the focus on my grand vision, what am I wearing in my photo ops or media appearances? Visualize how I want to look and feel. Write it down.

_____

_____

_____

_____

_____

_____

Based on my major achievement above, what accomplishments would the media highlight?

_____

_____

_____

_____

_____

_____

What do I think it will take for me to bring my vision into focus? What are the steps that will be required?

_____

_____

_____

_____

_____

_____

We're not finished with this topic. We will come back to it when we discuss your strategic networking action plan.

There are several critical factors that will directly affect your ability to network effectively. Your personal brand, as profiled in the next section, is the most important component.

PART II: PLAN

CHAPTER 4

BUILDING AND MANAGING YOUR PERSONAL BRAND

*All of us need to understand the importance
of branding. We are CEOs
of our own companies: Me Inc. To be in
business today, our most important job
is to be head marketer for the brand called You.*
—TOM PETERS

When it comes to advancement, doing a good job and mastering one's craft are not enough. You need a plan that helps to highlight your value and your contribution. Your personal brand has tremendous impact on how you are perceived by others. Let's face it, achievers want to associate with other successful people—those who have the drive, skills, character, and positive outlook to propel them to even higher heights in their chosen career or business.

Your personal brand is the embodiment of who and what you represent in the minds of others. It is the essence of your emotional, physical, interpersonal, and professional attributes that shapes your reputation and how others view you.

The term "brand" is often associated with physical products and services. Just as images come to your mind when you think of CNN, Disney, Starbucks, and Apple, your own name evokes reactions and thoughts in others. We often have images or pictures in our minds when it comes to leading product brands. For example, here are mine:

CNN—news leadership, international, timely
Disney—fun, visionary, creative
Starbucks—socially conscious, employee-friendly, bold
Apple—User-friendly, creative, service-oriented

Great product brands are not static. They are constantly raising the bar by adding new value and tweaking or expanding their product offerings. They are always learning and getting feedback from consumers. The same principles are required for building and maintaining your personal brand.

Your brand plays a critical role in your ability to advance. It is often a yardstick by which your are evaluated. Yes, there are those who believe in a meritocracy—a system in which people are selected for advancement based on their talent or strictly on the basis of some type of criteria. Such a system has no room for favoritism, biases, or politics as limiting factors for one's advancement. I'm not going to argue the point of whether such a system truly exists. From the perspective of my twenty-nine years in large corporations and organizations, I have not had an opportunity to observe such a system. Mind you, I have heard some leaders describe their organizations as meritocracies. Despite our best efforts, as mere mortals, we all have biases. And while some systems do a good job of implementing competencies and objective measures of performance, the human element is implicit in every process, whether in the ideation phase and/or the evaluation and administration phase. My point is that you must manage your brand and do your part to positively influence your environment and how others perceive you.

Perceptions of YOU do matter, as those views can help to advance or hinder your personal and professional agenda. According to the 2011 study by the Center for Talent and Innovation, a nonprofit research organization in New York, being perceived as leadership material is essential to being promoted into leadership positions. Most senior executives will tell you that executive presence is a key personal brand attribute. In a nutshell, executive presence means looking the part, and it is a judgment on one's ability to command a room and get people to listen. This may sound subjective, and I believe it is. For example, how would the CEO of a Fortune 500 company with a formal dress code assess the executive presence of the CEO of Facebook, Mark Zuckerberg? In a traditional formal environment, would he have been labeled unprofessional given his customary casual attire? Would female executives in a high-tech environment be less likely to advance if they wore jeans and T-shirts, or would they be accepted because of their talent and contributions to the workplace? My point here is that the concept of personal branding and how one is perceived and received by others is often subjective and situational.

When I think of well-known personal brands, names like Ursula Burns, Richard Branson, Meg Whitman, Mark Zuckerberg, Oprah Winfrey, Ken Chenault, Tory Burch, and Queen Latifah come to mind. These leaders have had significant influence in shaping corporate culture, technology, and entrepreneurship. In addition to leading successful enterprises, they are known and respected in their respective fields.

The goal of personal branding is to deliberately influence and shape the thoughts people have about you in ways that will advance your personal, professional, and business agenda.

Be thoughtful and strategic about your actions "live" and in cyberspace. Understand that you cannot control all aspects of how others perceive or receive you; however, you can positively influence those perceptions in most people.

Lessons from the Queen

Queen Latifah is an established celebrity. She is also a wonderful example of a woman whose career has been managed well and a person who has successfully developed and evolved her personal brand. I met Queen Latifah in 2007 and had the pleasure of introducing her to three thousand women at the Simmons Women's Leadership Conference. Here is a woman who has reached many pinnacles of success, and she was warm, gracious, and down-to-earth. She was welcoming to everyone she met. I was impressed with her easy personality and quiet confidence. She lived up to her reputation and continues to be a shining example of success for many women, regardless of their background. She has embraced change, stayed open to opportunities, and dealt with adversity effectively. She has built and sustained relationships that have helped her through many transitions. As a result, she remains grounded, authentic, relevant, and wildly successful. The remarkable thing about Queen Latifah is the skill with which she has made significant transitions throughout her life and her career. She's gone from being a high school basketball talent to a rap artist to the producer of her own record label to a Grammy award–winning artist. From there she went to TV and movies. She's a Cover Girl model. The list goes on. Clearly, hard work, perseverance, and business savvy contributed to her success. She has detailed many of her disappointments, setbacks, and obstacles in her book *Ladies First: Revelations of a Strong Woman.*

As someone who is focused on effectively creating and/or leveraging social and business networks, you must pay careful attention to your brand. Ultimately, your ability to connect meaningfully and evolve into an effective networker will rest largely on the strength of your brand. Managing our own personal brand is a job we each have. It is up to you to take the initiative, because the power to change things lies within you. The same principles that gave rise to Queen Latifah's success are available to each one of us and can be used to shape other personal brands.

Great product brands are not created in an instant, and neither are personal brands. Building and enhancing your personal brand should be viewed as a process. Personal branding is not just public relations and public personas. Those who have positive, sustaining personal brands are authentic. Think of the examples I mentioned earlier.

Your approach to building and strengthening your personal brand will vary depending on your environment. For example, most corporations have policies and protocols governing communications, social media, and public relations. Sending out a personal press release without the knowledge and consent of your company could be a violation of corporate policy, depending on the organization. The same is true for speaking to the media without organizational consent, posting on social media, and using other brand-building tools. Business owners and entrepreneurs have more options for building and enhancing their personal brands. It's advisable to evaluate what works best for the environment in which you live and work.

Let's start with some **brand-building tips** for entrepreneurs and corporate professionals.

Quality Matters—Do Great Work
You need to deliver a high-quality product or service. This is a basic requirement for building a strong brand. Whether you are running your own business or working for an organization, don't fall victim to mediocrity or—worse—poor quality. You want to be known for a high-quality work product. As a professional, you may think that this one is a given. Continuous improvement is the name of the game.

Stay Relevant
Keeping up with technological changes, finding new ways of engaging your stakeholders, and employing best practices within your industry are essential. For example, the definition of work, including where it's done and how it gets done, continues to evolve. In order to remain relevant, you too must evolve. For some people, a full-time job means forty hours glued

to a chair in an office building. It means being able to see, interact with, and stop by the offices of colleagues. Subordinates are expected to arrive at work exactly at (or before) nine o'clock and remain visible in the office environment until five o'clock or later (usually much later). The proliferation of technological advances, globalization, and cultural shifts, particularly among millennials, are some of the forces fueling the evolution of the traditional office environment. As leaders and managers, you want to acknowledge and tune into this and other trends. In order to be relevant, you must adapt and evolve your work practices.

Guard Your Reputation

Treasure and protect your reputation and your good name both offline and online. Take the time to become familiar with commonly used online business tools such as LinkedIn, Facebook, Twitter, or whatever the newest tool in your industry or community may be. Set permissions so that you are protecting the information you do not wish to make public. By now you have probably seen or heard about some of the online reputation killers related to Facebook postings. Bottom line: do NOT post it on Facebook or other personal social media if it could be damaging to your reputation. Those pictures from your island vacation where you're doing belly shots should *never* be posted online. You have no control over where they may end up.

Communication Matters

I have a dear friend who is a senior manager at a well-known hospital in the United States. She consistently sent e-mails to me that were casually written and peppered with incorrect grammar and punctuation. Did I mention she is in a senior communications role? I assumed that her lack of attention to grammatical details was due to the casual nature of our exchanges—until she requested a networking introduction. Sarah (not her real name) sent me an e-mail and requested that I forward it to one of my executive contacts along with her resume. I was stunned that the e-mail was casual, poorly written, and lacked punctuation—just like the rest of her casual communiqués.

I started to correct the errors but instead decided to call her and provide her with feedback. She was extremely grateful and sent me a well-written replacement e-mail to accompany her resume. Here is a highly accomplished, talented leader who had fallen into the bad habit of sloppy communications.

Eliminate your bad habits. Every e-mail, letter, card, blog, newsletter, voice mail, meeting, and presentation is a reflection of your brand. Communication is a key aspect of networking, so I have dedicated an entire chapter called "Communicating with Power" to the topic.

Be Visible

You may have the best products in the world or the best professional contributions in your field. If a great thing happens and no one knows about it, does it have the same impact on society and the world? Imagine if Apple had chosen not to promote the iPod. What if Oprah Winfrey had never aired her shows, her knowledge, and her unique perspective?

The reason we know about high-quality, impactful brands is that they were promoted. Notice I did not say *advertised*. While advertising is a paid form of promotion, few people have the financial resources of Oprah Winfrey. Promotional opportunities, however, are more accessible. In the business environment, they take the form of a memo, a speech, a panel discussion, a keynote presentation, an article, a performance plan, a resume, or a networking forum. Numerous forms of visibility are available, and you will have to assess what works best for you and your environment. Don't assume that people know the value of your contribution, product, or service. Seek opportunities to make your work visible to others.

Build Your Brand Equity

Be savvy about managing your image and seek to build your personal brand equity. Brand equity is the value that a company realizes from a product with a recognizable name as compared to its generic equivalent. Companies can create brand equity for their products by making them memorable, easy to use, and of high quality. These qualities often translate to higher market values for the company. Apple is a great example of a company with significant brand equity. As of May 27, 2015, the BrandZ Most Valuable Global Brands report lists Apple as the number-one most valuable brand with a brand value of $247 billion—an increase of 67 percent from 2014. Like great product brands, your personal brand has tremendous value. You want to build your brand's equity and good-will among your constituents—your associates, shareholders, stakeholders, friends, and equally important, your community. A tangible example of equity is a house. The owner can build or detract from the home's equity. New kitchens and baths will generally increase the home's value. Failure to maintain the home will decrease its equity. Engage in activities that will build your personal brand equity.

When you invest in relationships and improve your products and services to increase their value and give back to your community, you are building brand equity.

Give generously. It's a great way to be helpful and it provides a sense of satisfaction that you are uplifting and supporting others. You can give by volunteering in your community, mentoring others, donating quality products and services, and serving on boards. Not only are these the right things to do, they also help to improve the strength of your brand and contribute positively to your professional relationships. Serving is a great way to meet other like-minded people. Success in this arena can lead to a higher market premium for the brand called YOU.

The following is an excerpt from a 2011 interview with one of the most effective executives and master networkers I know, Marian L. Heard, on whether race plays a role in how professionals network.

Make yourself known within your organization and your community. Join key professional development organizations to meet others who share similar backgrounds or experiences.

Also, make sure that you are connecting to organizations that will provide opportunities to meet with individuals who have *very different* backgrounds and experiences. One of the best ways to do this is to volunteer. I spent over thirty years with the United Way system, the last seventeen in key leadership positions. Also, my other leadership positions were through national nonprofit organizations whose conferences, seminars, and forums provided extensive networking opportunities with key business, entertainment, sports, and political leaders, including the last six US presidents.

Volunteer opportunities should be viewed as a place to address serious social problems and give individuals a platform as well. "Do something good and feel something real" was an early theme for the Points of Light Foundation (now known as the Points of Light Institute), the largest volunteer advocacy and networking group in the world. Groups like this one are excellent vehicles for individuals to give time and money. It feels good to leave each meeting knowing that your efforts have helped those in great need.

Make sure that time is used wisely and that at the end of the day you can say that you made progress with your career and life's goals, but that you also took time to help someone else achieve theirs as well. (NMC Marian L. Heard, president and CEO, Oxen Hill Partners; retired president and CEO, the United Way of Massachusetts Bay; CEO of the United Way of New England)

Hone Your Positive Attributes
Know your brand attributes. Who are you? If someone were describing you, what descriptors would they use? I described Queen Latifah as "warm,

gracious, and down-to-earth." Observers may also say that she is talented, humorous, and wealthy. What are your brand attributes? In order to answer this question, you must be self-aware, and you must supplement that with input from others.

Next I will cover the essential tools that you must have in your personal branding tool kit. Take time to complete Making It Real for this chapter before you start that chapter.

Making It Real Action Exercise:
Defining My Personal Brand

Who am I? (Describe yourself.)

_____

_____

_____

_____

_____

What are my brand attributes? (List your best personal assets.)

_____

_____

_____

_____

_____

What are the descriptors (key words) I want people to use when they describe or think about me?

_____

_____

_____

_____

_____

How do I want to be viewed by others? What type of person do I want to be perceived as in the eyes of others?

_____

_____

_____

_____

_____

What steps must I take to shape that image?

_____

_____

_____

_____

_____

How do I think others would describe my personal brand?

_____

_____

_____

_____

_____

What attributes shape my reputation and how I think others view me?

- Generous
- Helpful
- Supportive
- Knowledgeable
- Technology savvy
- Emotionally intelligent
- Respectful
- Grateful
- Excellent writer
- Professional
- Creative
- Interesting
- Solutions-oriented
- Approachable
- Excellent orator

- Social-media savvy
- Other_____

Here are the areas I'd like to improve and any insights I've gained from my introspection (write them down):

_____

_____

_____

_____

_____

Making It Real Action Exercise:
Building My Brand Equity

What can I do to build my personal brand equity? (This includes how you are "striving to build brand equity and goodwill among your constituents— your associates, shareholders, stakeholders, and friends.")

_____
_____
_____
_____
_____
_____

What investments am I making in relationships? What improvements am I making in my products and services to increase their value and give back to my community?

_____
_____
_____
_____
_____

What am I offering that is of value?

_____
_____
_____
_____
_____

What activities am I doing to "give back" or "pay it forward"? (This can include such things as volunteering in your community, mentoring others, providing quality products and services, and staying true to your word.)

_____

_____

_____

_____

_____

_____

CHAPTER 5

YOUR PERSONAL BRANDING TOOL KIT

Recall my definition of a personal brand: *Your personal brand is the embodiment of who and what you represent in the minds of others. It is the essence of your emotional, physical, interpersonal, and professional attributes that shapes your reputation and how others view you.* Your brand assets are the tools that you use to represent your brand. Everyday you utilize branding such as your memos, agendas, and so on. Those are internal documents for business organizations and they are examples of your work product. Now I will address your external personal branding essentials. These are basics that you should have ready so that you can be proactive and be prepared for opportunities as they arise.

Important tools:

- Your story
- Resume
- LinkedIn profile
- Biography (Bio)
- Professional photo (headshot)
- Business card
- Thank-you cards

Your Story

Why you? With so many talented business owners, consultants, and executives out there, why would others want to network with you, hire you, or buy your products and services? What makes you special? What differentiates you from everyone else? What do you have to offer to the marketplace? In order to answer these questions, you must assess where you are and what you have to offer relative to others. In a crowded field of professionals, this is an area worthy of your time and attention. You already have the answers to a lot of these questions. Even so, it's a good idea to reassess where you are and, more importantly, to articulate your value proposition. You may also need to do some research to benchmark your personal work product and contribution against that of others. Let's say you are a best-selling author who happens to be a great speaker. You likely have a following and would be a draw for organizations wishing to hire you. Your best-seller status is a point of differentiation that can be leveraged to support your speaker fee structure. It is also a key way of describing yourself when you articulate your story.

"Your story" is not the same as your biography, although both can contain your key accomplishments. It is not your "elevator pitch," a term that is frequently used to describe how people can succinctly sell their ideas if they have only twenty to thirty seconds. A good elevator pitch should last no longer than a short elevator ride. The difference between your story and your elevator pitch is the focus. With the pitch, it's about the product or service that you are selling. Your story, on the other hand, is just as it sounds—it's about you. It can include your elevator pitch, but it should give people a sense of your authentic self. This is crucial for strategic networking. Business professionals are inundated by people vying for their time, dollars and ideas. The people who break through the clutter are those who have strong brands or a unique value proposition that can solve a business problem. This is also true for career advancement. Assuming that the core business competencies and skill sets are met, people hire people they like, people they trust, and people who will make them look good. This can be summed up as "protecting the brand."

Your story is what you choose to share about yourself to humanize you, connect with others, and cut through the stiff corporate rhetoric. Great speakers use storytelling all the time. Businesses are now catching on. People relate better to other humans, not to corporate mantras and spreadsheets. Yes, those things are necessary, but take a look at the corporate brands that are consistently at the top of their game. They are artful in storytelling, in engaging and connecting with people. This does not mean they won't make missteps, but brand authenticity leads to a quicker recovery. I attended a diversity awards ceremony where an executive from Starbucks spoke about its "Race Together" initiative—an effort by the company to get people talking about race. The executive admitted that the rollout could have been done differently. The backlash for the company was swift, but Starbucks held its ground, made adjustments, and continued the campaign. Starbucks drew on its positive brand equity as the company navigated through a challenging period. In contrast to what many experts expected, the stock value actually increased.

As a professional speaker, I often begin my talks with "An Unlikely Story." It is an opportunity for me to share my own journey. As an immigrant from the island of Barbados, I have lived in the United States much longer than I have lived in my homeland. Yet those early years and my experiences transitioning to America remain etched in my consciousness. They contributed to the person I have become. I grew up in poverty, a stark difference from the life I now lead, but that too shapes my thinking. It informs my decisions and the causes that I am passionate about. I continue to support organizations focused on education and poverty, because those two areas resonate deeply for me. Education was my ticket out of the cycle of poverty. Completing my master's degree in business administration was the fulfillment of one of my dreams, and I consider my sitting as emeritus board chair of one of the largest antipoverty agencies, Action for Boston Community Development, as one of the highest ways that I could have served. I can relate to those who are hungry, and to people who find themselves in desperate circumstances through no fault of their own. I can empathize, because I lived it.

People want to know the real you. You don't necessarily have to bare your soul, but give some thought to the ways in which you connect with your audience, your employers, and those whom you serve. Find ways to integrate and embed your story when appropriate. It needs to be authentic, so please do NOT make it up. You may never have been downtrodden, but hopefully you have helped someone along the way and can share from your own personal experience. Real stories strengthen brand authenticity. Although this is called "your story," clearly you may have many stories, so you don't have to limit yourself to one. I do recommend picking a theme, though—something you become known for and incorporate into your various speeches, conversations, and the like.

Making It Real Action Exercise:
Polishing My Story

Describe below what makes me stand out from the crowd.

_____

_____

_____

_____

_____

_____

What skills do I bring to the table?

_____

_____

_____

_____

_____

_____

What additional value do I add that is a positive differentiator from others?

_____

_____

_____

_____

_____

_____

My value proposition is: (What do I know or do that enhances my business or work environment?)

_____

_____

_____

_____

_____

_____

What is my story? What are the key experiences that help humanize me?

_____
_____
_____
_____
_____
_____
_____
_____
_____
_____
_____
_____

Your Personal Branding Tool Kit: Your Resume

Your Resume

Resumes are another opportunity to present the brand called YOU. Whether you are refreshing your resume or repositioning what you do, my key message here is have it ready, simplify it, and optimize it. Choose a simple, easy-to-read format for your resume. At some point in the process, you will need to send it electronically, so avoid complicated layouts. Search engine optimization (SEO) relates to how high on the list your content appears when keywords are entered into a search engine such as Google. You want to look up keywords for your industry and describe what you do in words that will help the search engines find you. This is also true for LinkedIn and any other online content repository.

Ensure that your resume is consistent with your LinkedIn profile and other online sources that you utilize. Employers, recruiters, and business owners routinely scan the Internet. While you may send your resume to them, expect that they will conduct a Google search to identify other content that appears on the web. Your brand is defined by the information you present as well as other communiqués, images and content that is linked to you. Conduct your own search, and be prepared to address any inconsistencies that may be present on the web. Update and correct the content sources within your control. If you discover inaccurate content that is not within your control, proactively address the issue. Better to tell your story than to have others make inaccurate assumptions.

As you acquire new skills, update your resume periodically so that you have it ready to go should an opportunity be presented to you.

Making It Real Action Exercise:
Refreshing My Resume

What actions must I take to update my resume?

_____
_____
_____
_____
_____
_____

Which keywords will I include in my resume to improve SEO?

_____
_____
_____
_____
_____

What information do I need to update and/or correct that could potentially damage my brand?

_____
_____
_____
_____
_____
_____

Your Personal Branding Tool Kit: Your LinkedIn Profile

Your LinkedIn Profile

LinkedIn is the world's largest professional network with 380 million users as of July 2015, and it's free—well, at least for the basic level it is free. It is a wonderful tool for networking, managing your network of contacts, and sharing professional content. Take the time to understand the tool, and stay abreast of updates and changes. LinkedIn is a "must have" in your personal branding tool kit.

My chapter on social media contains more information on LinkedIn, but here are a few quick tips for building your LinkedIn profile:

- Upload a professional photo.
- Complete the steps for achieving 100 percent profile completion.
- Read the professional community guidelines.
- Review and select the privacy settings.
- Actively engage by linking to others, updating content and by joining relevant groups.

Making It Real Action Exercise:
Building My LinkedIn Profile

I will take the following actions for my LinkedIn Profile:
(I suspect that most people already have a profile. If you don't have one, go to LinkedIn.com and create one now. If you have a LinkedIn profile, is it current? Review your profile and identify the things you need to do to make it current. These activities may include updating your photo, adding your current job, and requesting recommendations. Write them down)

_____

_____

_____

_____

_____

_____

I will check my LinkedIn profile for consistency with my resume and will update any sections that require attention. (Identify items that are currently out of sync between the two profiles)

_____

_____

_____

_____

I will modify my profile with keywords commonly used in your industry. This will help me with SEO. (List some of those terms here)

_____

_____

_____

_____

_____

My Professional Biography (Bio)

I've been told that professionals find this to be one of the most difficult documents to write. In the words of one woman, "I have three decades of experience. How can they expect me to fit it into a two-hundred-word summary?" Then there was the good doctor who promised to get her bio to me in time for a thought leadership forum I was organizing. She sent an eight-page document detailing her many accomplishments. It was impressive, but—really? Perhaps she didn't see the word limit? Truth be told, these two professionals faced a very common challenge. By definition, a bio is a short biographical profile. It is an important marketing tool, one that should reflect your personal and professional brand. People often think that only professional speakers or those who are being introduced at a public forum need a bio. The bio is often used in addition to the resume with regard to other opportunities, such as consideration for a board of directors seat, an e-introduction, nominations for awards, on websites, and for other professional opportunities. If marketing and writing are not your strong suits, hire an expert to write your bio. You will need your resume, key accomplishments, work items that differentiate you, professional credentials, awards, media appearances, if any, and a compelling story. Ideally, you want a long bio (up to one and a half pages) and a short bio. Depending on the situation, this can be as short as one hundred words. Be sure to point out the things that make you special or unique.

Here are two mini bios for men with similar backgrounds. Can you tell which person has a more compelling story?

Bio 1:
Armed with a four-year degree, John Brown went into the marketing field after he left MIT. He has over twenty-five years of experience and will lead the workshop on how to develop an effective marketing plan for your car dealership.

Bio 2:

Don Smith is a nationally recognized marketing expert with twenty-five years of experience. A graduate of MIT, Don created significant buzz when he launched the first JCMv.7X at the 2011 car show in Chicago. Don is the recipient of the 2014 Effie Award for the XYZ campaign. He will lead the workshop on how to develop break-through marketing plans for your car dealership.

How you describe what you do makes a difference. Be sure to showcase your unique qualities and attributes.

Making It Real Action Exercise:
Formulating My Bio

How do I want people to think of me, and what data exists to support this? How do I want my brand represented in the marketplace?

_____
_____
_____
_____
_____
_____

What differentiates me the most that is relevant to the audience I'm addressing?

_____
_____
_____
_____
_____
_____

What gives me credibility with this audience? (List awards, acknowledgments, credentials, degrees, ground-breaking research, programs, and so on.)

_____
_____
_____
_____
_____
_____

My company/employer would agree with my representation of my skills and expertise. (If you are not self-employed, be sure that you know your employer's policies. Bios are considered external documents and will include the name of your employer.)

I plan to have the following people review and/or approve my bio prior to publication (if applicable):

_____

_____

_____

_____

_____

_____

_____

_____

_____

_____

Your Personal Branding Tool Kit: Your Photo

Your Professional Photo (Headshot)

You've seen them on LinkedIn—the photo from Facebook with the person's pet or the dazzling party dress with lots of bling. Depending on your profession, those types of photos may have their place. For platforms such as LinkedIn, though, you need a professional photo (shoulders and up)—a headshot. You should have a digital, high-resolution (high-res), camera-ready format that can be e-mailed as needed. Make sure that the photo is flattering and that it actually looks like you. The headshot you took twenty years ago when you landed your first big job most likely needs an update.

Making It Real Action Exercise:
Assessing My Professional Photo

I have a recent professional photo that actually looks like me. (If you cannot say yes to this, please arrange to have your photo taken.) I will take the following actions to arrange for my photo shoot:

_____

_____

_____

_____

_____

_____

I've arranged to have a professional photo taken. The information is as follows (studio or individual):

_____

_____

_____

_____

_____

_____

I've updated my photo, and it looks like me: Yes _____ No _____

I plan to do this within the next month: Yes _____ No _____

Your Business Card

Your business card speaks volumes about you, your company, and your brand. Not having one with you also sends a message and could cost you an opportunity. Granted, some people intentionally do not carry cards, because they really don't wish to be contacted. They are likely not open to networking with you anyway, so move on. For those cards you do exchange, automate the process of electronically recording them. This will save you time and eliminate the usual "Oh, where did I put that card?" moment. For most users, a free card-camera app will do the trick. Personally I use CardCam to scan my business cards directly into my contact system while I'm still at the event. The app takes a picture and organizes the card's contact information into the appropriate fields on your smartphone. It's a great time-saver.

The type of business card you use and how you brand it will depend on a number of factors:

- Self-employed entrepreneur versus employed by an organization
- Best practices for your particular industry
- Budget
- Personal taste
- Planned usage of the card

If you are not self-employed, it's quite simple—check with your employer and adhere to its guidelines and brand standards. For those who are empowered to create or recreate their own cards, here are my suggestions:

- Choose a high-quality card stock.
- Select a design that reflects your brand. Better yet, have your designer create your card and adhere to the colors and other branding elements for your business.
- Ensure the display is simple and easy to read. Do not try to place all of the options below on your business card. Clutter will adversely impact your brand.

- Make sure you have all of the pertinent information on your card—your business name, your own name, your business address, phone number, and website address.
- The following are optional and dependent upon your type of business:

  - Photo
  - Twitter handle
  - Description of services (for cards with two sides)
  - Fax number
  - LinkedIn (your personal LinkedIn URL) e.g. www.LinkedIn.com/in/juliettemayers

Your Thank-You Cards

One way you can different yourself is to send a thank-you card or note. This gesture will help you stand out from the crowd, as physical thank-you cards are rarely sent these days. This too is an opportunity to express your brand, so be thoughtful about what you choose to highlight.

Making It Real Action Exercise:
Using My Business Cards and Thank-You Cards

Actions I will take to research business card automation tools/apps:

_____
_____
_____
_____
_____
_____

I will redesign my business card to better reflect my brand. The steps I plan to take are:

_____
_____
_____
_____
_____
_____

I plan to add thank-you cards to my tool kit and will keep them in a location where they can be easily accessed: Yes _____ Yes _____ (This is not an error—answering no is not an option!)

Who have I interacted with recently? Is there anyone in my network who should receive a thank-you card?

_____
_____
_____
_____
_____

Next best thing: A thank-you e-mail is also acceptable. While not as memorable, everyone still likes to see those two words, "thank you."

PART III: CREATE

CHAPTER 6

A MODEL FOR MANAGING YOUR NETWORK

Networking is the process of cultivating
mutually beneficial relationships
that increase visibility and expand opportunities.
—J. KEITH MOTLEY, PHD

Networking can be time-consuming. In order to increase your effectiveness, you must create or tap into networks that are both strategic and productive. Ultimately you want to spend your time on those activities that will get you closer to your goals while developing and sustaining relationships that are mutually beneficial.

Strategic networking requires development of a plan with actionable goals—but not all contacts have equal value. Not everyone will be aligned with the objectives that you are trying to accomplish.

You may be thinking "Just where am I supposed to find the time for this additional work?" After all, there is just so much energy to go around. And you're right. If you're like most professionals, you are already operating near or at capacity. The beauty of a strategy that you are passionate about is that it forces prioritization and realignment. You become energized by the clarity of purpose—a strategic focus. This means that you must learn to say no to low-value or no-value activities that do not align with your goals and yes to high-priority action items that move you toward your objectives.

Consider the following model for managing your network. There are numerous ways of looking at this, so find a framework that works for you and modify it to meet your needs.

Strategic Networking Model

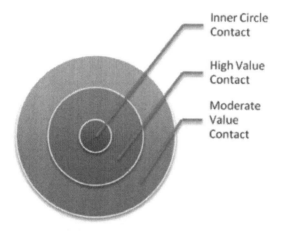

Inner Circle Contact

High Value Contact

Moderate Value Contact

Inner Circle Contacts (ICCs)
—Small in Number and Highly Influential
ICCs are people with whom you have a deep, trusting relationship that has stood the test of time. You can discuss highly sensitive subjects with them and know that your conversation will be confidential. They care about you and have been there for you through the tough times. They are your cheerleaders and bring opportunities to you. They provide access to places and resources. These are your advisors, mentors, and friends who truly have your best interests at heart. They know your goals and dreams and support them wholeheartedly. They have nominated you for awards, provided

references, counseled you those times you were stuck, and generously given of their time to help you succeed. They are authentic, and they give you constructive feedback and encouragement as needed.

Managing Your ICC Network

- Treasure and nurture these relationships; do not take them for granted.
- Actively think about how you can be helpful to them; perform random acts of kindness.
- Be sincere and authentic in your dealings.
- Praise them and use them as examples in forums that are beneficial to their business.
- Refer business to them.
- Recommend those who are public speakers for speaking engagements.
- Share your vision and goals with them.
- Schedule time to connect with them in person, one on one, at least twice a year.
- Maintain contact throughout the year via e-mail, cards, and calls.
- Forward information that may be of interest to them.
- Extend invitations to important events.
- Return their calls immediately.

Making It Real Action Exercise:
Managing My ICCs

List below the names of my Inner Circle Contacts (ICCs)

1. _____
2. _____
3. _____
4. _____
5. _____

Managing My ICC Network: Below is the list of actions I can take to manage my ICC network effectively. (Check off those steps you will take to accomplish this with my connections. Feel free to add others.) Quality and follow-through are important, so I must choose actions that I can commit to do.

- Treasure and nurture these relationships. Do not take them for granted.
- Actively think about how I can be helpful to them, and perform random acts of kindness.
- Be sincere and authentic in my dealings.
- Praise them and use them as examples in forums that are beneficial to their business.
- Refer business to them.
- Recommend those who are public speakers for speaking engagements.
- Share my vision and goals with them.
- Schedule time to connect with them in person at least twice a year.
- Maintain contact throughout the year at least six times via e-mail, periodic calls, and letters.
- Forward information that may be of interest to them.
- Extend invitations to important events.
- Return their calls, e-mails, and texts immediately (within twenty-four hours)
- Other_____

High Value Contacts (HVCs)
—Larger Pool of Contacts than ICC with a High Degree of Influence

HVCs are people with whom you have a trusting relationship. You may have worked with them for many years. Perhaps you went to college with them or sat on a board together. They may be people with whom you go to church. HVCs respect you, and you have very good rapport with them. You share information and resources, and they know enough about you to provide a job or business reference. You share a mutual respect.

The relationship is not as deep as with your inner circle; however, you can count on these people as professionals, colleagues, and friends. They "have your back."

Managing Your HVC Network

The management of HVCs is very similar to ICCs; however, ICCs have a higher priority when it comes to your time and the level of information shared. From a practical standpoint, connecting one-on-one with this larger number of professionals would be quite challenging. Consider networking forums, holiday parties, and group events as a means of bringing together this tier. Your HVCs do not have to be at the same place at the same time. Communication and the sharing of information are keys in maintaining engagement and brand visibility for you.

Making It Real Action Exercise:
Managing My HVCs
List some of the names of my High Value Contacts (HVCs)

1. _____
2. _____
3. _____
4. _____
5. _____

Managing My HVC Network: Below is the list of actions/options I can take to manage my HVC network effectively. Check off those actions I will take to accomplish this with my connections. These tasks are in addition to the ones I will perform for my ICCs.

- Treasure and nurture these relationships. Do not take them for granted.
- Actively think about how I can be helpful to them, and perform random acts of kindness.
- Be sincere and authentic in my dealings.
- Praise them and use them as examples in forums that are beneficial to their business.
- Refer business to them.
- Recommend those who are public speakers for speaking engagements.
- Maintain contact throughout the year via e-mail, periodic calls, and letters.
- Forward information that may be of interest to them.
- Extend invitations to important events.
- Return their calls and e-mails within forty-eight hours.

Moderate Value Contacts (MVCs)
—Largest Pool of Contacts with Potential
for Advancing to a Higher Tier

MVCs are people with whom you have a connection. It may have come from a networking event, a business forum, your child's school, or a conference. For MVCs, the relationship may be relatively new, or you may have known the person for years, but your goals and interests do not necessarily align (at least not at this time). You may have mutual respect but don't necessarily have the depth of relationship at which you would be comfortable putting your professional reputation on the line for that person. Your goal with MVCs is to stay connected; however, you are not to invest the same level of time and effort as you would for your HVC or ICC contacts.

Your MVC network still has value, though, and occasional opportunities may arise for you to lend support for an initiative that does not pose a high risk to your reputation.

Making It Real Action Exercise:
Managing My MVCs

List below the names of my Moderate Value Contacts (MVCs). This is a larger pool of contacts than my ICCs and HVCs, people with whom I have a connection, perhaps from a networking event, a business forum, my child's school, or a conference. A lot of people in my LinkedIn list may fall into this category. List some of my MVCs below.

1. _____
2. _____
3. _____
4. _____
5. _____
6. _____
7. _____
8. _____
9. _____
10. _____

Managing My MVC Network: Below is the list of actions/options I can take to manage my MVC network effectively. Automation tools such as group lists, e-mail marketing tools such as Constant Contact, and social media tools for business such as Facebook Pages can help me with this. These contacts are an important tier in my network and could very well migrate to another tier, so I must employ the same quality of communication and branding. Check off those actions I will take to accomplish this with my connections. These tasks are in addition to the ones I will perform with my ICCs and MVCs.

- Actively think about how I can be helpful to them, and perform random acts of kindness.
- Be sincere and authentic in my dealings.
- Maintain contact throughout the year via e-mail, periodic calls, and letters.

- Forward information that may be of interest to them.
- Provide periodic updates (e.g. e-mail and LinkedIn).
- Extend invitations to group forums and networking events when relevant.
- Return their calls and e-mails as my schedule permits (utilize automation tools as much as possible).

CHAPTER 7

YOUR BOARD OF DIRECTORS

You are well on your way to advancing your business objectives, so how can you be more effective? It's time to rev up your strategic networking plan. As you gain greater influence and visibility, more people will place demands on you. You must have a laser-like focus on your goals and your time commitments. It is time to zero in on high-value networking activities such as those noted earlier in chapter 6. This does not mean dismissing or disrespecting other relationships—it just means that you spend most of your time and energy on those activities that are likely to yield high returns and ones that are aligned with your plans.

Recruiting Your Personal Board of Directors
As you examine the various players in your network, you should identify the ones you think would be open to serving on your personal board of directors. This team is particularly valuable for entrepreneurs and business owners. The areas of expertise represented will be dependent on your grand vision and where you will need support. For some people, this may be a one-on-one "as-needed" team of experts; for others it may be a more formal process, particularly if your business is organized as a corporation. In either case, you want the initial outreach for your board to be one-on-one. This is an area where you should identify the "What's in it for her him or her (WIIFH)?" You will want to have a game plan before your initial outreach. Depending on your needs and the time commitment involved,

it may be appropriate to pay a stipend. In many cases, experienced mentors and ICCs will donate their services as long as the role does not infringe significantly upon their time. Be up-front about the required time commitment so that you get the right resource.

For those who are not entrepreneurs, the concept of the board of directors can also be applied to your career. Identify the mentors, experts and in some cases, peers, who can help to advise you. It is generally a good idea to have multiple people with whom you can strategize. Don't limit yourself to one organization. Seek the counsel of others outside of your company and your industry. In so doing you will have diverse perspectives and you will also broaden and deepen your network.

As you think through your board-of-directors membership, be strategic. You want people who have held leadership positions and who bring unique talents into your circle. Look for chiefs—people who can bring expertise on key functional areas whether or not they have the official "C-suite" titles. This includes the following:

- Chief Information Officer (CIO)
- Chief Human Resources Officer (CHRO)
- Chief Financial Officer (CFO)
- Chief Legal Officer (CLO)
- Chief Marketing/Communications Officer

Actively Chairing Your Personal Board of Directors

Part of a board's responsibility is to ensure that the organization and its resources are focused on its vision and mission. The board's role is to help you vet ideas, offer assistance, and provide you with its expert input relative to the direction of your enterprise. Effective recruitment and leadership of a highly functioning board is essential; so is the ongoing management of those relationships. A great place to start is with people you know who have the required skills and competencies. Organizations also exist that specialize in helping entrepreneurs put together these types of boards. Depending on your industry, level of complexity, and organizational-structure requirements, you may need to hire a professional firm to help you with recruitment.

Making It Real Action Exercise:
Creating My Board of Directors

To create my personal board of directors, I need to start with the list of people who are already in my strategic network, particularly my ICCs and HVCs. Once I've completed this first exercise, I can move to the next one, where I will identify my empty board seats and whom I must recruit into those vacancies. (List possible names as well as tactics you will employ to get them involved on my board.)

List below the names of my current contacts who can fulfill the following board slots by bringing expertise to my network on key functional areas whether or not they have the official "C-suite" titles:

- Chief Information Officer (CIO) Contact Name: _____
- Chief Human Resources Officer (CHRO) Contact Name: _____
- Chief Financial Officer (CFO) Contact Name: _____
- Chief Legal Officer (CLO) Contact Name: _____
- Chief Marketing/Communications Officer Contact Name: _____

List below the names of contacts I need to recruit to fill my vacant positions and the tactics I will employ to recruit them to my board of directors:

- Chief Information Officer (CIO)
  Contact Name: _____
  Tactics to get them involved: _____
  _____

- Chief Human Resources Officer (CHRO)
  Contact Name: _____
  Tactics to get them involved: _____
  _____

- Chief Financial Officer (CFO)
  Contact Name: _____
  Tactics to get them involved: _____
  _____

- Chief Legal Officer (CLO)
  Contact Name: _____
  Tactics to get them involved: _____
  _____

- Chief Marketing/Communications Officer
  Contact Name: _____
  Tactics to get them involved: _____
  _____

  Contact Name: _____
  Tactics to get them involved: _____
  _____

CHAPTER 8

CREATING YOUR STRATEGIC NETWORKING PLAN

Thinking through the elements of your strategic networking plan was the first part of the process. Next, you need to document your plan. Write it down, and you will be more likely to get it done. In this chapter, I will walk you through the development of your networking plan.

Earlier I discussed our three networking tiers: ICCs, HVCs, and MVCs. Networking tiers are not static, and neither is your plan, so it is entirely possible for an MVC to evolve into an HVC and vice versa. Structure and plan your communications to stay connected and visible to your network.

You have determined your grand vision, you're working on brand "You," you have stratified your network and you have identified your personal board of directors. It's now time to establish your goals. Let's say you want to grow your technology business—your small enterprise that you hope to grow into a thriving entity within five years.

As you think about your business or your career, it is important that you do so holistically. Think through the following twelve questions:

1) What is your 5-10 yr. vision for yourself and your business (do both personal and business)?
2) What are your values—those non-negotiable principles by which you live and govern your life?
3) As you contemplate development of goals, think about all dimensions of your life, as they are interconnected. You may find it helpful to create goals and sub-goals for categories such as health, family, spiritual, financial, business and career and community
4) What are your top priorities?
5) How are you currently spending your time and with whom?
6) Are your activities and commitments aligned with your personal and professional objectives?
7) Are you making progress towards making your vision a reality?
8) What metrics do you have in place to assess your progress on areas of your life that are important to you?
9) Do you have a networking strategy?
10) What changes should you make to increase the effectiveness of your networking?
11) How have you contributed to advancing your community?
12) Are your personal and professional relationships productive? Are you spending time with the right people?

Start with Your Vision

Previously you created you personal vision statement—Your Grand Vision. Imagine the future for you and your business. Take a look at the grand vision you documented in part I of this book ("Dream") and use it as your starting point. If you haven't yet completed this exercise, you can do so in this section. In it, you imagine that you are on the cover of your *favorite business or career* magazine five to ten years from now and the cover story is about the achievement of your grand vision (see Making it Real).

For illustrative purposes we will use XYZ Technology Company.

Vision for XYZ Tech company:

To be the leading technology partner for the STEM industry in MA.

XYZ Technology's SMARTER Business Goals: **S**pecific, **M**easurable, **A**ttainable, **R**ealistic, **T**ime-bound, **E**thical, and **R**esourced (source: www.achieve-goal-setting-success.com).

The goals of your technology company are as follows:

- Achieve $5 million in revenue by 2020 through targeted focus on high-growth STEM (Science, Technology, Engineering, and Math) companies.
- Evaluate four partnership opportunities each year, and implement at least one to accelerate profitable growth of the business.
- Complete modification of IT architecture by end of 2016 to ensure flexible, scalable options for larger clients and to maximize future acquisition opportunities.
- Implement brand building strategy by February of 2016 to increase visibility and attract prospective clients

XYZ Technology's CEO's Values-Driven Goals:

Health:

- Maintain optimum health by jogging three miles and/or attending Zumba classes at least four days a week
- Maintain commitment to eating whole foods by planning daily meals at home and work

Family:

- Plan and budget for week-long family vacation by January each year to avoid scheduling conflicts and to ensure quality time with the entire family
- Document key school-related activities for children on work and home calendar and by the beginning of each school year

Spiritual:

- Prioritize prayer and meditation by spending the first half hour of each day on these activities
- Attend church services weekly

Financial:

- Review and update wills, insurance, trusts and healthcare proxies when necessary by April 1st each year.
- Contribute a minimum of 10% to family savings, investments and emergency fund each pay period.

Business (see other biz goals for XYZ Technology above):

- Achieve $5 million in revenue by 2020 through targeted focus on high-growth STEM (Science, Technology, Engineering, and Math) companies.

Career:

- Attend at least one industry conference annually.
- Review and update on-line profiles – LinkedIn, Resume, Bio and Blog, by January 20th of 2016.

Community:

- Continue to teach pro-bono technology work-shop for high-school students at local high school thru May of 2017
- Attend and serve at annual Community breakfast June of 2017 to raise funds for technology upgrades at local high school.

You will notice that XYZ Technology Company completed goals for the business and values-driven goals. I encourage you to prepare both sets of goals. The business goals will be executed by the employees of XYZ Tech with oversight from the CEO. By documenting both sets of goals, the CEO brings focus to all of the key goals that support the long term vision. The complete set of goals is also a reminder that energy and planning are required not just for the business goals, but for the overall health of the family. Another benefit of the holistic approach is the integration of plans can be more easily aligned.

The next step is to identify the people and resources required to bring the vision to fruition. One of XYZ's business goals is to increase visibility and here are sample initiatives for that goal:

XYZ's Tactics to Increase Brand Visibility

- The company joined the chamber of commerce
- The CEO is scheduled to speak a high profile regional STEM conferences
- The CEO was published in Harvard Business Review
- XYZ Technology won a "Best Company" award
- XYZ Technology sent a related press release out to all of its clients and posted the honor on its company website, its LinkedIn profile, and its Facebook page

- The company partnered with Get Konnected, a popular networking event, to host a networking forum at its waterfront location

You can follow a similar approach to ensure for your grand-vision, your goals and identification of initiatives. Be sure to complete Making It Real.

Making It Real Action Exercise:
Crafting My Strategic Networking Plan

1. What is my grand vision for myself and my business? Think five to
    ten years out. (Copy your earlier responses from part I here so that
    you will have everything in one place.)

    _____
    _____
    _____
    _____

2. What are my values—those nonnegotiable principles by which I
    live and govern my life?

    _____
    _____
    _____
    _____

3. What are my SMARTER goals? (Think about all dimensions of
    your life, because they are interconnected. Creating goals and
    sub-goals for each of the major categories that you value may be
    helpful.)

    a. Health

        _____
        _____

    b. Family

4. _____
    _____

a. Spiritual

5. _____

_____

_____

a. Financial

6. _____

_____

_____

a. Business and Career

7. _____

_____

_____

a. Community and Politics

8. _____

_____

_____

Now that I have identified my goals, I need to prioritize them.

9. What are my top priorities? If I were forced to pick no more than five goals, what would they be?

_____

_____

10. How am I currently spending my time relative to my goals and priorities? How much time do I spend on noncore activities (those activities that do not support my goals)?

_____

_____

11. Are my activities and commitments aligned with my personal and professional objectives? *(Don't forget those dearest to me.)*

_____

_____

12. My goals should be structured so that they are not all front-loaded (year one only). Am I making progress toward my longer-term goals?

_____

_____

13. I will use the following metrics to monitor my progress:

_____

_____

14. My networking must be aligned to support my goals and objectives—short term and longer term. I plan to do this by making the following adjustments to my professional, affiliations, memberships and networking forums:

_____

_____

15. I will make the following changes to increase the effectiveness of my networking:

_____

_____

16. How am I contributing to advancing my community?

_____

_____

17. Are my personal and professional relationships productive? Am I spending time with the right people? I plan to make the following changes:

_____

_____

CHAPTER 9

ASK FOR WHAT YOU WANT

Leverage the relationships you have established to access the inner circle of other decision-makers and movers and shakers with whom you want to connect. You have to be very strategic in who you ask. What is your expected outcome? How does it align with your grand vision and with the areas of interest for those in your network?

I found that learning how to ask for help did not come easy for me. I grew up in a culture where asking for help was viewed as a weakness. I can recall the anguish my mom endured when she was forced to ask for help to feed our family. You may recall from my opening story – my solo journey to America. My mom later made the transition to the US along with my sisters and she had difficulty supporting our family. For her, this was a shameful position. Many years later, she still viewed the experience as a deep failing, even though she had developed the skills necessary to advocate for herself and her children. This was the context and frame of reference that seared my psyche. I've since come to learn that self-reliance, discipline and doing great work are not enough. Asking for help and enlisting the support of allies, mentors and sponsors is necessary for accelerating ones growth trajectory. As I mentioned previously, it is also essential that professionals nurture and protect the brand called YOU.

Asking for what you want means that you are relying on others to meet a need—some level of dependence is involved. For some, this may signal a deficiency or vulnerability, while others may have been conditioned to routinely make the ask. Regardless of which camp you are in, this is a skill that differentiates the "Haves" from the "Have Nots." As you think about your grand vision, big dreams require lots of "asks" and in some cases, very big "asks." Our focus here are on strategic asks with the purpose of advancing your career and growing your business.

Let's look at a specific example:

> When I started Color Magazine, I wanted to meet a key person who had started other publications, so I went to an event where he spoke where I could meet him. When I arrived at the dinner, I found the location of his table. He was at the table with his wife. I went over to the table, introduced my self and started a conversation with his wife. I then asked her permission to speak to her husband about help for my business. I spoke to him briefly about the idea and asked whether we could meet for coffee to discuss the concept in more detail. He said yes. In this case, everything worked perfectly.
>
> In another instance, I requested time with someone with whom I already had an established relationship. She is a successful business owner and I really admired her. I sent her an email letting her know about my plans to launch the business and requesting her help. I also let her know that I admired her work and requested just fifteen minutes of her time to get insights on a specific approach that I was considering. She did not respond to my email. A few weeks later, I saw her at an event and she introduced me to someone and referenced content from the email, so it was clear that she had read it. She did not acknowledge my request; nor did she offer to help. In this case, I moved on and reached out to the next person.
>
> Don't be afraid to ask for help. Find a select group of allies who provide you with a zone where you can be vulnerable to seek advice and support. In addition to networking, you have to keep

learning. Come from a place of interest. It is important to be open to other professionals and what they do. You must listen, listen and listen. As a professional, you have to be a robust balance of strategy, reflection and action. You have to listen, learn and do. (NMC Josefina Bonilla, CEO and Chief Marketing Officer of Color Media Group, LLC.)

Asking for Career Advancement

I find that people can more readily apply this concept of asking to a Sales environment or for a business enterprise–less so for professional career advancement. To a large extent, there are a lot of professionals and executives who feel strongly that they should receive recognition and opportunities on the strength of their contribution to the organization. We have all heard stories of people who have been literally tapped on the shoulders, taken into the office and have been given big promotions, significant bonuses and the like.

As you read this book, some of you are holding firm to the concept of the organizational meritocracy. Surely "they" will see and recognize your value. You shouldn't have to ask, because John didn't ask and he has not made the kinds of sacrifices nor the level of contribution that you have made to the organization. Your performance appraisals have been stellar, you have put in the time and you are a team player, so surely your day will come. Right? Possibly, but why not take control of your own destiny.

What you may not know is that John golfs with the boss on the weekends. Their children are in the same soccer league, they have mutual friends outside of work and the boss has a comfort level with John. He trusts John. Furthermore, John has documented his contribution to the organization, is highly visible as a result of his volunteer board work, and he has articulated what he wants. Oh yes, while they were on the golf course, John asked for a promotion and substantiated why he should have one. He actually prepared a discussion document that he went over with the boss the following week.

It didn't happen immediately, but the boss knew what John was after and factored it into the team reorganization. The boss was armed with the data he needed to make the case for John, because John was proactive in providing it to him. This minimized the work that the boss had to do to persuade HR and armed him with the facts and figures he needed to have the conversation with his peers and the other senior executives. The data answered the question "Why John?" So you are right. John was tapped on the shoulder and brought into the office; however, a lot transpired behind the scenes both in terms of networking, strategic visibility, documenting of contributions and relationship management and sponsorship.

I'm not suggesting that all promotions happen this way. I did want to bring home the point that there are a lot of other factors at play when it comes to professional career advancement. As you ascend to the senior ranks, competence is assumed, so it is critical that you adopt a "continuous improvement mind-set," know your market value and network, network, network! Ask and your wish is more likely to be granted. There is no down side to asking, other than your personal perceptions of rejection. What's the worse that can happen? An outright "no." Even that response is a gift; particularly, if you are lucky enough to have the person share their rationale. You may not agree with it, but the feedback can be powerful and will help you to assess your range of options.

Be Clear about Your Ask
What is that you want? If you have done the work of completing your grand vision and your goals, you will have a great starting point for identifying requests.

This is not the time for vague objectives such as "I want to grow my business." Of course you do. You need to articulate what specific help your company needs. Are you looking for a referral, an endorsement, a contract bid, technical assistance, financing, or board-member recruitment for your company? Maybe you need help refining your goals.

Let's say you want to grow your small technology company and you need help executing on your accelerated growth goals. You are looking to attract a Chief Marketing Officer for your personal board of directors. You should be prepared to articulate why your company is unique. What makes you different from the other businesses? Why do you think you can actually achieve your revenue targets in the time frame that you have set for yourself? What specific support is essential to expedite your growth? Perhaps you have a patent for a new technology that you plan to license, and you are looking to obtain expert advice in this area. You may also need some board members with specific expertise to help guide your company through this next phase. Whatever you need, crafting your story and *then* making "the ask" are more likely to get you results. Practice your message, but do not deliver a rote, over-rehearsed script. You must display sincerity, positive energy, and confidence. Make sure your request is well thought out and succinct.

Address WIIFH
Make sure you ask about the other person's priorities, challenges and opportunities. She will be even more receptive if you can tie her interests to your interests. As a leader, you must also think through the WIIFH, a variation on "What's in it for me?" If you are not already familiar with her work, do your research. Talk to others who know your prospective CMO. Read industry publications where she is referenced. Google her! What are the things that would help *her* succeed in advancing her agenda? Who are your mutual contacts? How can you utilize your expansive network to help her achieve her goals? Is there a creative way that you can leverage your contact.

What If the Power Scales are Uneven?
You may not always be in a position to offer something of equal significance to the person from whom you seek help. You should still ask about their challenges and priorities and try to identify the WIIFH. The process

is ongoing, so continue to scan the environment for opportunities to help, send invitations to events and activities that may be of interest and speak highly of your contact with others who may be in a position to help them. The small deeds can sometimes add up to more value than you may think. Lastly, but most importantly, say thank you. Acknowledge the help that you have received, and make it a point to let the person know the impact of their actions on your work and on your business.

Making It Real Action Exercise:
Ask for What you Want

After reviewing my grand vision and my goals, the area where I need help are:

_____

_____

_____

_____

_____

My plan for reaching out is as follows:

_____

_____

_____

_____

_____

My main objective is to:

_____

_____

_____

_____

_____

I have clarity about what I want. It is (feel free to include multiple asks):

_____

_____

_____

_____

I've given some thought to the interests of my contacts and have identified a few areas where I can be helpful:

_____

_____

_____

_____

_____

CHAPTER 10

A WORD ON CAREER ADVANCEMENT

The old adage "out of sight, out of mind" holds true for career advancement opportunities as well. Having a strong personal brand and doing a great job are great starting points, but a lot of other factors are at play. It is very important that you understand what is considered success for your organization. If you are in the market for a job at a new company, this still holds true. Even with a great personal brand, strong performance, and relevant credentials, the human factor is still at work. As I noted previously, people want to work with people they like, those whom they can trust, and those who can get along well with others. Career advancement relies heavily on "who knows you," particularly in the middle to senior ranks. Hiring managers may rely heavily on their networks, people they trust, and may not have a conversation with you until very late in the process, if at all. They may get recommendations from their golf or tennis buddies, a fellow board member, one of their peers, or a person in HR whom they trust. The important thing here is that these people may not be part of the official recruiter's list or networks.

This informal outreach through personal networks can be a disadvantage to some; particularly women and minorities, who may not be plugged into the social networks of executive leaders. While the percentage of women and minorities in the workplace has increased, the upper echelons of most organizations remain dominated by men. As it relates to advancement, a recent study of Wall Street analysts revealed that men tend to be evaluated on potential, while women are judged on their actual performance. This is old news; however, these findings could help to explain the continuation of the gender gap when it comes to career advancement.

Men and women who feel that they are outside of the social networking construct can take action. One concrete thing you can do is to expand your "known" quotient. Make sure your work is visible to your peers to your subordinates and to decision makers and influencers. Another is to leverage your mentors and existing networks to get introductions to decision-makers. Don't limit yourself to one organization. Change happens and the impact to you cannot always be foreseen. Exposure through networking, speaking at conferences, serving on boards, and articulating your story, are all ways in which you can increase your known quotient.

The following quotation provides further food for thought on the keys to growth and advancement:

> There are multiple factors that contribute to success, including a certain amount of luck and timing. One of the keys to growth and advancement is doing an outstanding job. As one's career develops, formal and informal networks can be very helpful.
>
> Work hard. Work smart. There is no substitute for hard work. Develop, build, and expand your networks. It's as much about what you can give as about what you can take.
>
> No one formula fits everyone in every situation. It is important that you be yourself. Don't try to be someone you're not. Authenticity is important. Develop confidence in who you are and what you have to give. Be persistent in terms of fulfilling career and business aspirations—it's an important quality. (NMC Paul Guzzi, Chairman, Chairman, Citi Center for The Performing Arts)

Your personal board of directors can play a critical role in helping to identify opportunities that are aligned with your goals and objectives. Be sure to keep them in the loop on your progress within your current role. When you decide to pursue other opportunities, communicate your plans to your ICCs and engage them early in the process.

Stay Connected to ICCs and HVCs

Whether you are considering a career change or simply looking to maximize options for advancement, make it a point to stay connected with ICCs and HVCs.

Relationships are complex and nuanced; they need to be nurtured. This is true for familial networks, business alliances, and partnerships. Building and maintaining productive relationships require deliberate actions that will build your brand, support your personal and professional objectives, and provide mutually rewarding experiences.

Here are some further thoughts on the importance of leveraging your brand to increase your networking effectiveness:

Your strategy will likely be more successful if you have developed a strong personal brand. Develop your own personal brand. Think of yourself as a product to be managed, advertised, developed, and sold. At a certain point, we have to understand the competition and find ways to differentiate ourselves. It can't just be bravado. You have to be willing to put yourself out there and take opportunities to speak in public or write for an association magazine.

- Get known as an authority in your own right.
- You can get really invested inside the organization. Don't stay inside too long. You need to see and be seen by the outside world.

- Be very clear about your long-term goals, and arrange your short-term goals with those in mind.
- Stay true to your dreams and work toward those. Take it in "bites."
- Stay attentive to where you fit within the organization and in your job.
- Take advantage of opportunities for public appearances and conferences that are relevant in your field.
- Attend at least two or three charity events per year.
- Take the initiative to start a new role if you have outgrown your job. Don't stay too long in one role. (NMC Helen Drinan, president and CEO, Simmons College)

Helen's advice reminds us of the importance of having clear goals and providing specific action steps for enhancing networking effectiveness.

PART IV: ACHIEVE

CHAPTER 11

21 Tips to Help You Take Action

All progress takes place outside the comfort zone.
—*Michael John Bobak*

Sustained effort and a commitment to seeing your grand vision through are required to achieve success in realizing your dream. The best way to get started is to get moving now. Don't cling to the security blanket of your comfort zone. Say goodbye to excuses. Take the steps necessary to activate your plan today and make networking a habit.

Research shows that it takes twenty-one days for individuals to form a new habit. To help you with the integration of networking into your daily life, I have identified 21 tips. I suggest that you work on at least one tip per day. Some of the tips require actions that are on-going, so you will have an opportunity to repeat the cycle.

Tip 1: Determine areas of focus
Review your strategic networking plan and you goals. Identify one or two goals that you plan to work on within the next month.

Tip 2: Engage in at least one networking activity per week
Instead of wolfing down lunch at your desk while you check e-mails and read reports, what if you dedicated at least one day a week to having lunch with a colleague or someone in a different industry you would like to get to know better? When done consistently, just this one change will substantially expand your network.

Tip 3: Tier your network
Stratify your existing contacts into ICCs, HVCs, and MVCs. Approach your stratification with your prioritized goals in mind. The stratification process may take a few days or perhaps weeks depending upon the size and complexity of your contacts.

Tip 4: Identify key networking opportunities
Check out available business networking opportunities in your industry and within your organization. Don't overlook the ones that are already within reach, such as those on community boards on which you serve. If you are not well versed on available opportunities, ask someone who knows.

Tip 5: Attend at least one networking event
Target at least one networking event per month. Ideally, you should have one professional or industry membership for your business or organizational affiliation. Before attending events and forums, do your homework. Determine who will be in attendance—which organizations, consultants, influencers, and vendors you should connect with at the event. Establish some objectives for your attendance and/or participation. Use your strategic networking plan as a reference.

Tip 6: Mentally prepare yourself

Think through what you wish to accomplish when you get to the event. Visualize—what would success look like for you? Write it down.

Tip 7: Invite a friend or colleague

It's perfectly fine to have a friend or colleague accompany you to your event. This is likely to make the experience more comfortable. Just don't spend the entire occasion with the person you already know. Step out of your comfort zone and get to know other people.

Tip 8: Maximize conferences, professional organizations and forums

Register to participate in at least one conference per year. Ideally, you want to strive for thought leadership by presenting your work or speaking at the conference. Whether you are a presenter or participant, there is tremendous value in connecting with like-minded professionals at conferences and forums. Additionally, these are great visibility opportunities to showcase your brand and your work.

Here are some thoughts on the value of professional organizations:

Getting to know people in professional organizations was key. I found that becoming active on a board was a good way to get involved. I was very active on the board of The Boston Human Resources Association. Through that organization, I got to know a lot of entrepreneurs. When I got to the point of starting my own business, I had the relationships and sounding boards to assess whether I should proceed. Ultimately, this helped me to make a career choice and solidified my decision. (NMC Martha R. A. Fields, Fields Associates)

Tip 9: Do Your Homework

Leverage the power of search engines to enhance your networking prowess. Use search engines to research speakers and known attendees in advance of the forums you plan to attend. The information you learn could then be used to spark an informed conversation with those in your network. Most people love to talk about themselves and their accomplishments. By doing your homework, you will be in a better position to have a deeper connection beyond the elevator pitch, name and title exchange.

Tip 10: Create a financial plan

Establish a budget for your networking strategy. For example, it may take twenty-four networking luncheons or coffees (two per month) for your entrepreneurial pursuits to be sustained. The person who makes the invitation generally picks up the tab, so factor these and other costs, such as conferences, dinners, communications, business supplies, airfare, and so on, into your budget. Research the costs of your plan, and identify the appropriate funding sources. You don't want your fabulous dream to turn into a financial nightmare!

Tip 11: Expand your "known" quotient

It's okay to start with people you know, but the productivity of your network will come from who knows you. It is quite possible that you have a substantial contact list of people you have met over the course of your business career. How many of those people actually know you well enough to be able to vouch for you or recommend you? Do they really know you as a person? Do they know your capabilities? Your objective should be to focus on being known to the people who are core to your strategy. When you increase the number of people who really know you and your outstanding work, they can become your ambassadors, cheerleaders, and in some cases, your ICCs. Building and managing your brand will enhance your "known" quotient.

Advice to women:

Performance trumps everything. Identify opportunities to tout your achievements and value to the organization at the highest levels. It's a continuous process. Women should seek out strategic initiatives within their organizations and volunteer to work on projects to distinguish themselves from others. Identify a sponsor and ask them to recommend you for highly visible projects. Once you have performed well, use it as an opportunity to network with senior executives by inviting them to lunch or by scheduling an early morning coffee in their office. The glass ceiling will only shatter if economic pressure is exerted by purchasing goods and services only from those companies who expressly demonstrate and acknowledge the worth of women in the suite and boardroom. (NMC Linda Watters, vice president, government relations, John Hancock)

Tip 12: Diversify your network

It's human nature to associate with people with whom you have a lot in common, who may be in the same social circles and who have shared characteristics – ethnicity, gender, race, professional affiliation and the like. Many of us tend to have much stronger ties within our own race when it comes to networking, socializing, and participating within religious affiliations. Globalization and demographic shifts are leading to an increasingly diverse America. Get to know people who are different from you. In our increasingly global world, these relationships will be a source of strength.

To be an effective networker in this evolving world, you should do the following:

- Be deliberate about including people from different backgrounds, races, ethnicities, ages, and genders in your inner circle. This process takes time; you won't be able to check it off your list in one day. It requires being consciously and deliberately inclusive.

- Act as a convener among influential people. In Vernon Jordan's memoir, *Vernon Can Read*, one of the things that struck me was his commentary about inviting others and not always being the one to be invited. While this might seem like a small thing, there is significant power in being the convener, particularly when it comes to business and career transactions. The opportunities for convening people are plentiful. You can do this during the course of your workday by seeking input from others, facilitating dialogues, or hosting a substantive meeting. Don't meet for the sake of meeting. By bringing people together, you have an opportunity to influence the agenda and accelerate connections among your constituents while positively building your brand. This is true on the social side as well. Going to the homes of friends and attending birthday parties, dinners, and social clubs can be a lot of fun. You get to skip the expense and the cleanup. Yes! You may not be in a position to reciprocate in a similar fashion, but do find a way to include those who consistently extend themselves in a venue of your own. It could be at a restaurant, picnic, gospel concert, or whatever fits your style and your budget. The point is to move from receiver to giver and convener.

Tip 13: Be proactive in your outreach

Once you have identified the people with whom you want to connect, reach out to them. You can do this via e-mail, LinkedIn, a card or handwritten note. Despite the popularity of online technology, a brief handwritten letter (that includes your contact information) sent through snail mail is often more impactful. It is a subtle message that you are someone who has taken the time, effort, and forethought to reach out. Understand that the rapid pace of business has placed a significant strain on professionals and leaders. Although they may be well intentioned, you may not get a response or acknowledgment of your communication. Gone are the days of leaders surrounded by layers of administrative support and assistants to return the long list of calls. Whether or not you get a response, you have increased your brand equity by adding to the positive impression of your professional brand. With this simple gesture, you have already separated yourself from the pack. Here is an example of a note you can send to introduce yourself prior to meeting:

Dear Juliette:

Congratulations on your second book and on your appointment to the US SBA's Federal Advisory Board. As an entrepreneur and aspiring author, I look forward to your upcoming presentation at the Massachusetts Conference for Women.

Warm Regards,
Ivan X. Johnson
President, Phenomenal Events

With this simple note, Ivan has accomplished several things:

1. In a nonintrusive way, he has introduced himself.
2. He has given Juliette a heads-up that he will be at the upcoming conference.
3. Ivan took the time to find out something about Juliette. This gesture can be quite flattering to the recipient.
4. He has also introduced his company, Phenomenal Events.
5. Ivan has made a positive deposit to his personal brand equity account.

Tip 14: Add value
Think of common interests or potential ways in which you can strike a win-win connection. Ideally, you want to identify something that will

help to advance your business and/or career while supporting the goals and objectives of the person with whom you are trying to build a relationship. Don't worry if the exchange is not mutually beneficial; not every connection will be equal. However, you should strive for this goal whenever possible.

Tip 15: Keep your word

Do what you say you're going to do. If you can't, follow up with your contact, and let them know why, *before* you are late delivering on your commitment. In the workaday world we live in, it is easy for some people to let things slide. Your word is a test of your personal brand strength. Have you ever purchased a product or service where you were lavished with attention and praise before the sale? The salesperson made you feel like a million bucks. His promise, however, was not fulfilled because the equipment broke not long after you got it home. You called the sales representative and customer service repeatedly. After many wasted hours and lack of follow-up, you gave up or wrote a letter to the salesperson expressing your disappointment and asking for his assistance. No response.

Would you purchase another product from that sales representative? Would you refer your friends? No. Absolutely not! The trust and the brand equity are gone. Don't let this happen to you. When you make commitments to your network, keep your word.

Tip 16: Attend culturally diverse networking venues

Your plan should include a variety of venues and a breadth of diversity. With the rapidly changing demographics, many organizations are seeking opportunities to expand workforce diversity and to participate in culturally diverse events and forums. In Boston, Get Konnected is one such forum.

Get Konnected is the largest multicultural networking forum in Boston, Massachusetts. Eight years prior to starting Get Konnected, I created Kaleidoscope, the first multicultural directory in Boston for professional, personal care, and business resources. By working with many of the affinity groups in Boston, I realized that there was a need to bring diverse groups together. Originally, Get Konnected was a social experiment to address some of the social challenges. It is a low-cost, professional networking event open to all cultures. It is not intended to replace affinity groups, as these groups still serve a very important role for professionals. (NMC Colette A. M. Phillips, president and CEO, CPC Global and founder of Get Konnected)

Tip 17: Present your brand

Even if your business is small, you should have a summary and marketing brochure that describes your capabilities. Your personal branding toolkit is a great place to start. Make the necessary changes to present the best YOU.

Tip 18: Practice

Like any new skill, repetition builds mastery. Practice the art of inquiry. You want to show interest in the other person with whom you are network-ing. Also practice your introductions. Who are you? What do you do? What is it that you wish to convey (succinctly)? Share your story.

Tip 19: Be authentic

Authenticity means not hiding who you are. I've had friends scrub their re-sumes and bios to remove any trace of anything that may potentially reveal their ethnicity. While I understand wanting to tailor one's resume for the particular opportunity, you should assess whether you really want to work for an organization or leader who is offended by your race, ethnicity, or sexual orientation. You want to go where you will be celebrated!

Tip 20: Plan your meetings and calls

Just as you would not walk into an interview unprepared, you should have a clear idea of what you hope to accomplish in your networking calls or meetings. It's also a good idea to let the other person know your objectives so that you can avoid wasted time and effort.

Tip 21: Build relationship equity

Your relationships in the workplace and marketplace are essential for business effectiveness, but don't stop there. Reach across industries. Similar to brand equity, you build relationship equity when the value of what you have appreciates. Invest in your relationships by making deposits of time, helping others, and staying in touch with peers, service people, former bosses, teachers, mentors, and advisors. The deposits may not always go to the person who made the investment, meaning you may make deposits with people who may not necessarily be able to reciprocate at that time. It's not always a direct exchange. You do want to establish a reputation as one who seeks to help and give to others. Over time, you will develop a reservoir of goodwill.

Here's how networking led to my first career opportunity:

> I started my professional career with GE Capital back in the eighties. During that time, Jack Welch was at the helm of GE, and the process for the Management Development Program (MDP) was extensive and highly competitive. GE was the *crème de la crème* of leadership development, and a spot in the management program, with its on-the-job sink-or-swim management rotations in multiple states, was a highly desired trainee position. As a participant in the MDP program, my management rotations were in North Carolina, Ohio, and Connecticut. This experience provided a great launching pad for my career.

In retrospect, my selection into the program is a lesson in the power of networking. During my senior year at Northeastern University in Boston, I attended a seminar with a speaker from GE; I was impressed. Immediately following the talk, I approached him, congratulated him on his presentation, and asked about opportunities at GE Capital. He informed me that they were not recruiting at Northeastern at that time. It was then that I eloquently delivered my elevator speech, letting him know that I was a marketing honor student who had completed internships at IBM, RJR Nabisco, and The Boston Globe; I worked three part-time jobs; was impressed with all of the wonderful things I heard about GE Capital, and was interested in GE Capital's leadership development programs. I asked him to take my resume for consideration, and he agreed. I requested a business card so that I could follow up with him, and I did. After two solid days of interviewing at GE Capital's headquarters in Stamford, Connecticut, I was hired into GE Capital's Management Development Program. The rest is history. (NMC Juliette C. Mayers, president and CEO, Inspiration Zone LLC)

Preparation Matters

The outcome of my GE Capital example above would have been very different had I been ill prepared, unknowledgeable about GE, and afraid to market myself. I also read the presenter well. The fact that the GE executive engaged students and was willing to talk after his presentation signaled to me that he was someone who could be helpful. Clearly, his company had an interest at the university, or he would not have accepted the speaking engagement and certainly would not have stayed around after his presentation.

Look around you for real life examples of people who are making things happen and doing so in ways that are inspiring. Create your own tips from those real world examples. The key to mastery is practice.

Making It Real Action Exercise:
Actions I Will Take

The actions that require my ongoing attention are (write down the tip # and any thoughts that resonate with you relative to the particular tip):

_____

_____

_____

_____

_____

_____

_____

_____

_____

_____

_____

_____

_____

_____

_____

_____

_____

_____

_____

_____

_____

_____

_____

_____

_____

_____

_____

_____

CHAPTER 12

THE ROLE OF SOCIAL MEDIA

The proliferation of new technologies is rapid. Just when you think you're up to speed with one tool, another one pops up. It's like the amusement park game of whack-a-mole in which you're constantly trying to anticipate where the mole will pop up and get there in time to whack it. In this case, the "whack" is the adoption of new social tools. In this chapter I provide you with an overview of the most commonly used tools for business and share with you advice from guest experts including Angela Pitter, CEO of LiveWire Collaborative.

Winning with Social Media

One of the beautiful things about the Internet is that it can provide a level playing field for those who invest the time to understand and use it wisely. The proliferation of social media has provided an opportunity for us to move beyond the offline social mastery to online business and economic empowerment. Additionally, social media can help accelerate offline ventures and serve as a low-cost networking tool.

Social media lets people of all backgrounds and ethnicities into the conversation. It is a technological and networking revolution, as it shifts the balance of power from professional publishers and communicators—who often serve as "gatekeepers" of information—to individuals. In this digital world, these tools allow access to those who take time to leverage the expansive opportunities. Without specialized training, small businesses can create a website, record videos, write and publish content, and much more. These powerful tools can accelerate brand building and ultimately fuel growth and effectiveness.

There are numerous social-media venues; however, given our objective of advancing careers and growing businesses, only the most widely used (as of the writing of this book) are mentioned in the following pages. Regardless of the medium, you must do the work of defining your goals and objectives first. Once you do this, focus on the tools you need to help you execute your plan.

From a networking perspective, LinkedIn is my go-to social-media tool.

LinkedIn Facts (source: LinkedIn.com)

About LinkedIn

- LinkedIn operates the world's largest professional network on the Internet with more than 380 million members in over two hundred countries and territories
- Roughly 1 million new members join LinkedIn every week. This is equivalent to one new member per second.

Tips for Using LinkedIn

Don't wait until you are looking for a job to use LinkedIn. Be proactive. Use this powerful tool to connect and stay in touch with others in your profession as well as your cross-industry contacts. It's a great tool for your ICCs, HVCs, and MVCs as well as for new connections.

If you are in the job-search mode, LinkedIn can accelerate your search. Here are some tips for maximizing the power of LinkedIn:

- Complete your LinkedIn profile at http://linkedin.com.
- Be sure to keep your profile updated. Use the privacy settings strategically. In the member profile section, you can customize what, if anything, LinkedIn publishes about you. Take the time to familiarize yourself with these options. To expand your knowledge, LinkedIn has several options for education, including webinars on how to get the most out of your LinkedIn account.
- Join LinkedIn groups based on your areas of interest. LinkedIn makes it easy to connect with affinity groups, and you also have the opportunity to create your own group and invite others to join.

Using LinkedIn to Find a Job
Personal branding guru Dan Schawbel, author of *Me 2.0,* has the following suggestions on finding a job using LinkedIn:

1. Establish your profile by copying the contents of your resume into the various LinkedIn fields.
2. Think about all of the keywords that a recruiter might use to find someone with your expertise, and then spread those keywords throughout your profile.
3. Edit your public profile to include a custom URL for your brand name, such as http://www.linkedin.com/in/danschawbel.
4. Your headline should position you for the career you want, not the job you have or had. It shouldn't read "Marketing Associate at XYZ Company." Instead, use keywords and a positioning statement, such as "SEO (search engine optimization expert) for small companies."
5. Get a recommendation from a previous job by giving a recommendation to one of your contacts first, without asking for anything in return.

6. Add three links to websites, blogs, or profiles that best represent your work professionally, using the full name of each website. For instance, use "Mark's Finance Blog" instead of just "blog."
7. Join LinkedIn groups, and start your own group based on your interests, either professional or personal.
8. If you have a blog, add the Wordpress or Typepad application to your profile to highlight the last few posts you've written.
9. Import your contacts from your other social networks and e-mail database so that you have a foundation to build upon.
10. Search for specific jobs on LinkedIn, and try to locate people in your network who can forward introductions for you.

As LinkedIn is a professional network, Dan suggests you accept everyone as a new contact. By doing so, your second- and third-degree contacts will multiply as you build your first-degree contacts.

LinkedIn has numerous features. Some of them are as paid, premium services for job hunting. But even without the paid features, you can use the following strategies to increase your visibility on LinkedIn:

LinkedIn Groups
Identify the affinity groups within your industry, and determine which ones are likely to be most useful. If you have an idea for a group that is not represented, start one, and invite others to join the group. You can share information, ask questions, and identify opportunities to engage with others.

Leverage Links
Use the links on your profile to showcase relevant organizations, such as those in your community work, professional services, or personal website.

Get the Word Out

If you are actively looking for a job, let your network know. If you are currently employed, you obviously don't want to put out an "all-points bulletin" about your search. Here's where you may want to take advantage of LinkedIn's premium services to connect with recruiters, get notifications, and manage job opportunities. Don't underestimate your friends. There are numerous stories of people who got leads from simply linking to others. Here is one of them:

Networking to me is actively connecting with people to give and get information, primarily to further business or professional aspirations, whether it's through professional organizations or through online tools like LinkedIn, Facebook, and Twitter. It can be in formal settings at conferences, business meetings, workshops or seminars, or informal settings such as coffee shops and restaurants. Believe it or not, one of my most active networking venues is my hair salon. I always encounter high-achieving, professional women. In this relaxed environment, women are often eager to engage in networking conversations. Stylists themselves are often great connectors since they serve clientele from a wide range of professional settings. My college alumni association is another great source of networking opportunities. These organizations are a great source of people who are in my field or related fields and are great for identifying professional opportunities, training, and resources.

Networking has played a significant role in my career success. I can safely say that my last two job opportunities that I accepted were found through networking. One was through my graduate school alumni organization. My most recent job came as a result of linking to a friend of mine on LinkedIn.

Within an hour of linking with him, someone in his network sent me an inquiry regarding a role at his company.

> Networking has also played a big role in helping me find roles internally within a company. Just as in the external market, available jobs are not always posted on the jobs board. Even if they are, there are often candidates who are already short-listed for the role. I've reached out to the hiring manager well before a job is posted or early in the posting process; that has helped me get a leg up on my competition. (NMC Cheryl Ginyard-Jones)

Facebook Facts (source: Facebook.com)

About Facebook
"Founded in February 2004, Facebook's mission is to give people the power to share and make the world more open and connected. People use Facebook to stay connected with friends and family and to discover what's going on in the world and to share and express what matters to them."

The company develops technologies that facilitate the sharing of information through the social graph—the digital mapping of people's real-world social connections. Anyone can sign up for Facebook and interact with the people they know in a trusted environment.

Users
As of June 30, 2015, Facebook had over 1.49 billion monthly active users (83 percent of them outside of the United States and Canada).

Product
Facebook the product is made up of core site functions and applications. Fundamental features to the experience on Facebook are a person's home

page and profile. The home page includes the news feed, a personalized feed of the user's "friends'" updates. The profile displays information he or she has chosen to share, including interests, education, work background, and contact information. Facebook also includes core applications—photos, events, videos, groups, and pages—that let people connect and share in rich and engaging ways. Additionally, people can communicate with one another through chat, personal messages, wall posts, "pokes," or status updates.

Technology
Facebook is one of the most trafficked sites in the world and has had to build an infrastructure to support this rapid growth.

Platform
Facebook Platform is a development platform that enables companies and engineers to deeply integrate with the Facebook website and gain access to millions of users through the social graph. Facebook is a part of millions of people's lives all around the world, providing unparalleled distribution potential for applications and the opportunity to build a business that is highly relevant to people's lives.

Privacy, Safety, and Security
Facebook has always focused on giving people control over their experience so that they can express themselves freely while knowing their information is being shared in the way they intend. Facebook's privacy policy is TRUSTe certified, and Facebook provides simple and powerful tools that allow people to control what information they share and with whom they share it. More information can be found at http://www.facebook.com/privacy/explanation.php. From its beginning, Facebook has worked to provide a safe and trusted environment by, for example, requiring that people use their real names. Facebook also works with online safety experts around

the world and has established a global safety advisory board that it consults with on safety issues. More information can be found at http://www.facebook.com/fbsafety and http://www.facebook.com/security.

Using Facebook to Advance Your Business

You are probably familiar with Facebook's profile pages. Facebook also has business pages. You can post videos, events, updates, photos, and other applications. Set up your Facebook page at www.Facebook.com/pages, and click the "create a page" button. It's that simple.

Social-media branding is equally important as offline branding. Dan Schawbel, personal branding guru and author of *ME 2.0,* has these five tips for social networking sites:

1. **Discover your brand before you communicate it.** You need to identify what you want to stand for: your mission values, brand attributes, and how you've differentiated yourself within your industry. It's hard to reflect on what your strengths and long-term goals are, but without identifying them, you will end up rebranding yourself many times without a sense of purpose.

2. **Protect your brand by reserving your full name everywhere.** You need to own your digital property before someone else does. This includes your domain name (yourname.com) and your full name on social networks such as Facebook, Twitter, YouTube, and others that are relevant to your brand. For example, if you're a real estate agent, you should join Active Rain (www.activerain.com). Also, you can have more control over the Google search results for your name because all these networks rank high in Google.

3. **Set up a system where you can manage your online reputation.** To keep a pulse on your brand, you should set up a comprehensive Google alert (Google.com/alerts) for your name. This way, anytime your name is mentioned in a blog post or news article, you're aware of it. You should also use Facebook search and BoardTracker.

com for discussion forum mentions. If you neglect observing and responding to brand mentions, you risk negative word of mouth, which can travel very fast online.

4. **Choose a single picture, name, motto, and theme—and use it consistently.** As with a corporate brand, consistency is key, which means you should have the same presence everywhere, online and offline. Take one professional headshot of yourself, and use it as your avatar on social networks, on your blog or website, on your business cards, and other places where your name is mentioned. If your name is Matthew but you want to be called Matt, then use that name everywhere, and don't change it. You can have a motto or tagline just like Nike or another brand, as long as you use it repeatedly. The same goes with your overall theme, including font, color, and style.

5. **Publish content so that people get a sense of your voice, not just the facts on your resume.** A resume isn't a differentiator anymore. Now you need an active voice online by publishing content. When you publish, it helps you to become more visible and credible and to connect with more people. Innovative companies want people with fresh ideas and different thinking, which is why participating in online forums is so important these days.

Here is a perspective on online and offline networking:

> Online networking is growing rapidly. There is a bigger distinction in traditional versus nontraditional networking among older versus younger professionals. Older people put more stock in offline networking. While there is increased adoption of online networking, most decisions are still made through offline networking. If there isn't a personal connection, online networking will be treated with a healthy dose of skepticism. You need a blend of the two—both offline and online. Network regionally and nationally. Make the investment in yourself. (NMC Colette A. M. Phillips, president and CEO, CPC Global and founder of Get Konnected)

Twitter (source: Twitter.com)

About Twitter

Twitter is an online social networking service that enables users to send and read short 140-character messages called "tweets." Registered users can use and post tweets. Twitter's mission is to give everyone the power to create and share ideas and information instantly, without barriers. Here are Twitter's stats as of June 30, 2015:

- 316,000 monthly active users
- 500,000 tweets per day
- 77 percent of Twitter users are outside the United States

People use Twitter to discover what's happening in the world right now, to share information instantly, and to connect with people and businesses around the globe. With hundreds of millions of users and over 500 million Tweets being sent each day, there is a great opportunity for businesses to reach a global audience of new and existing customers.

No matter what type of business you are — from a large retailer to a freelance designer; from a B2B software provider to a mobile app company — you can use Twitter to build meaningful connections with a relevant and engaged audience. These connections can lead to actions across a network of loyal customers for your business.

As with Facebook and LinkedIn, you will need to create a profile for Twitter and familiarize yourself with privacy policies. Some of the benefits cited by business who regularly use Twitter are:

- Simplicity – The 140 character maximum ensures that updates are kept short and encourages simplification of messages
- Rapid feedback
- Can create quality network
- Brand Visibility

There are numerous resources to help you learn the basics and maximize the utility of the tool. If you are just starting out, you just spend some time on Twitter.com. I also found Twitter Power 2.0 by Joel Comm to be helpful resource.

For those who are beyond learning the basics, Angela Pitter, CEO of Live Wire Collaborative has a primer on how you can power up your brand with social media.

5 Ways to Power Up Your Brand with Social Media
Angela Pitter, Founder and CEO, LiveWire Collaborative

The 2015 Pew Internet Project's research was recently released. One of the major findings is that 65% of adults now use social networking sites—a nearly tenfold jump in the past decade. Seventy-one percent of online adults use Facebook. The social web has clearly become woven into in the fabric of our personal and business lives.

How we appear online is an essential component of our persona and who we are in a digital world. Therefore, it is critical that modern professionals take control of their personal and business brand online. The content created on social media helps to defines your brand and is amplified across social networks as people discover and share information. Here are 5 tips to help you expand your brand on social media.

1. **Drive Brand Awareness via Cross-Promotion**
   Do you have active audiences on multiple social media profiles? According the recent Pew Study, this phenomenon is more prevalent than ever with more than half of Internet users (52%) using two or more of the social media sites measured (Facebook, Twitter,

Instagram, Pinterest, and LinkedIn). Given this fact, it is in your best interest to cross-promote your sites whenever and wherever possible.

When using cross-promotion, start with the pages you own— namely, your blog or website. The number one idea is to use the social share buttons. Make sure that your sharing tools are prominently displayed on your home page. If your site includes an email subscription box, ensure you social media icons are visible in that area so that users can easily connect with you via social media. The point is that you need you have your social media share buttons in multiple locations on your website. In fact, Founders and CEOs often neglect to include the LinkedIn share button on their "About Us" page to enable clients and customers the ability to connect with them on a professional platform. Why is this important you ask? Remember on LinkedIn you can only request recommendations (i.e. testimonials) from connections.

On blog sites, include the floating sidebar share buttons, so that the buttons remain visible as the user scrolls down to explore your site. It doesn't end here. Also include social media share buttons on each blog post. If Twitter is one of your primary social sites, not only include the icon widgets, but also incorporate the Twitter Embedded Timeline on your site or blog. Check out Twitter's developer's page. There are a lot of custom options you can implement including displaying feeds based on hashtags.

As you write your blog, think about those ideas that you want your readers to quote over and over again. How about making it easy for them by building in "Click To Tweet" to promote, share and track your content. And the best part here, this tool is free! There are also WordPress plugins such as Inline Tweet Sharer to encourage visitors to share your tweetable content.

Facebook remains the most popular social site worldwide. It offers various opportunities for promoting links to all of your social profiles. You can start by adding links to your social sites in the "About" section of your Facebook page. You can also incorporate Custom Tabs for each social network. Popular third party apps like Woobox or Tabsite easily connect your other social accounts to your Facebook page. Once integrated, a fan can not only view your Pinterest page for example, but experience it entirely as you can like the pins and follow the page without leaving Facebook.

Beyond Facebook, on each social site, make sure that you're linking to your other social media accounts on the Contact, About Us and Bio sections: These visitors are already reaching out to you; give them another way to connect with you. This works best when your social media usernames are consistent. This means that your account handles and usernames must match your personal or business name. Avoid abbreviations. This way, when others (clients included) search for you by name, they will actually find you.
Finally it doesn't pay to be shy about linking to your social media accounts. Do so in your newsletter, email signature, blog, etc. The final point worth repeating, use these social icons everywhere, not just at the very bottom of your email newsletter!

2. **Use Hashtags to Drive Results**
   Straight from Twitter business basics - "A **hashtag** is any word, or phrase without spaces, beginning with the # symbol. People use hashtags to organize conversations and make it easier to find all content related to a given topic. Click on a hashtag to go directly to the search results for that term." Since hashtags are indexed by search engines, using the same custom hashtag on different platforms helps to optimize organic results for your brand or business. While hashtags are a great tool for searching and finding content, they're not unique, you cannot "own" a hashtag.

The power behind the hashtag comes from your ability to find one that will help to amplify your brand. In fact, you're better off creating a hashtag strategy that includes a series of hashtags that will become recognizable to your audience over time. Don't overdo hashtags. With the exception of Instagram where interactions are highest on posts with 11+ hashtags, typically only one or two hashtags are needed. According to Buddy's Media Research, when more than two hashtags are used on Twitter, engagement is likely to drop off an average of 17%. Twitter's own research found individuals can see 100% increase in engagement when using hashtags and the data for brands is 50%. For Pinterest, the jury is still out. Some research has shown that Facebook posts without hashtags outperform those with hashtags. Your results will vary, so use these data points as guidelines and always perform your own tests with your content and your audiences. You should follow the KISS principle. In this case, keep it short and simple. Here are three tools that I would recommend to help you kick-start your hashtag strategy:

- **Twitalyzer** to see the most common hashtags being used by your competitors, influencers and brands you admire.
- **Topsy** to determine the popularity of each hashtag. Find a balance between overly used hashtags and those less recognized.
- **Tagboard** if you are using a custom hashtag for your community. Here you can register custom hashtags and include a description to make it clear that you've claimed it. Now when someone searches your hashtag on **Tagboard**, your description will pop up.

3. **Use your Cover/Header/Background photo like a Billboard**
   You only get one chance to make a good impression and your background (also called cover or header photo, depending on the social network) can be the most important and powerful online branding

tool. Think about it: this photo is not only the first image viewed on your page, it's the largest piece of real estate and it's free.

This area can be used in multiple ways. Clearly your own branding including logo, website and contact information should be an integral component of your background. Use it to show the benefits of your product or service or to promote new services or soon to be released products. On Facebook your cover photo can even be used to build your email list. Getting ready to kick off an event or be a keynote speaker at an event? Well this is prime space for promoting events.

Don't keep the same background photo for too long, change your photos periodically and have them reflect trends to demonstrate that your brand is relevant and timely. There's no real formula for how often you change your cover photo, monthly tends to work well as it follows the holiday calendar which is convenient for retail or ecommerce based businesses. Otherwise, at a minimum change your background quarterly.

Background images are different sizes on each social network. On Twitter your header photo is 1500 x 500 pixels and your Facebook cover photo is 851 x 315 pixels. The recommended image size on Google+ is 1080 × 608 pixels and the best size for a background photo for a LinkedIn personal profile is 1400x 425 pixels. Try using tools like **Canva** or **PicMonkey** to create your background. These sites have pre-designed templates already optimized for each social site.

4. **Maximize Brand Impact with Visuals**
   What's that saying? "You can't be a one trick pony?" That is definitely the case with social media. While a picture is worth a

thousand words, a video is worth a thousand pictures! Rapid brand expansion is more likely to occur with a multi-media strategy.

Some brands integrate visual social platforms like **Pinterest** into their core marketing strategy. For example, Nordstrom with roughly 4.4M million followers (as of the writing of this book) uses Pinterest as a promotional tool. The store highlights its most popular pins by 'pinning' them in the stores. Pinterest is a great marketing tool for anyone in food, crafts, home décor, and the fashion industry. In fact food is the number one category, so if you're a foodie, chef, caterer or restaurateur, then Pinterest should be a central component of your branding strategy.

Videos are another option that have become an extremely useful tool social sites. Facebook recently introduced native video – literally uploading videos from your desktop. When you upload natively, the video can actually auto-play in a newsfeed. How's that for an attention grabber? If you link a YouTube video to your Facebook post, the image is smaller and those posts have significantly less reach than posts that include videos uploaded natively.

According to **SocialBakers**, a popular site for social media analytic tools, brands posted 20,000 more videos on Facebook than they did on YouTube in December 2014. In the last year, videos have taken off on Instagram and Twitter as well. On Instagram, AdWeek cites examples of increased followers once major brands implement videos. For example, Victoria's Secret more than doubled its audience from 4.2M to 10.5M and Nike skyrocketed from 4M to 12M within a one-year period (April 2014 to 2015).

On Twitter you can significantly increase the number of shares and follows by creating educational content in a visually appealing manner. Videos are best used to educate or inform an audience. In fact, event coverage is another major use of video. Twitter video drives greater interaction by involving followers in your event if they can't be there. Like Facbook, Twitter video stands out in the rapidly moving feed so you can garner more attention from your followers to build trust with your audience.

Finally, we cannot leave out LinkedIn. Was your keynote speech videotaped or perhaps you or your business was featured on a TV show segment? Stand out from the crowd, by linking these sessions to prominent areas of your profile such as the "Summary" or link these videos to the "Publication" or "Project" sections of your profile. Look up Brynne Tillman, CEO Social Sales, on LinkeIn for examples of how this can work for you. Lastly, consider investing in a video bio that can be integrated into your "About Us" page on your website and on your LinkedIn profile.

5. **Use Humor to Boost Your Brand**
   Heard this joke before?

"I have to breakup with you. We've connected on so many platforms—Facebook and Twitter—but I just don't feel LinkedIn." - Derek Kessinger

One of the most effective ways to market is to evoke emotion. If you want your customers to associate good feelings with your brand, then humor is an excellent addition to your social media toolbox. It makes your brand memorable, invites conversation and expands your social presence via shares, likes or retweets.

A funny story grabs the attention of your audience and has staying power. Using humor will help you be memorable, driving greater brand recall and helps you to define your personality. It also creates stronger emotional ties with your audience and makes it easier for you to connect and build a tightly knit community.

Each social channel has a different tone. As with all marketing campaigns, the key to success is to know your audience and what's appropriate for your brand and the networks you're using. While use of humor is common on networks like Twitter and Facebook, you'd approach a professional site like LinkedIn with caution.

In summary, take control of your personal and business brand online with these 5 power tips. Social Media is not just one-to-one, it's one to many! Use the tools not only for people to discover you, but also because your brand will be amplified across social networks as people discover and then share it with their networks!

Making It Real Action Exercise:
My Plan to Power up my Brand on Social Media

I've identified the following actions that I will take to leverage social media:

_____

_____

_____

_____

My timeframe for implementing the actions I've identified is (include deadline for each action identified):

_____

_____

_____

I need help in the following areas:

_____

_____

_____

In looking ahead towards my longer term goal, I plan to power up my (or my company's) use of the following tools:

_____

_____

_____

_____

CHAPTER 13

COMMUNICATING WITH POWER

*The way we communicate with others and with ourselves
ultimately determines the quality of our lives.*
—*ANTHONY ROBBINS*

Communication is the cornerstone of building a brand, establishing credibility, and building trust. The "how" is as important as the "what" when it comes to communication. In the age of e-communications, it is easy to fall into a pattern of rapid responses rather than thoughtful, purposeful exchanges. This chapter provides insights on the "how" for achieving breakthrough communications.

Activate and align your communications plan for yourself and for your business. Your personal communications plan consists of ways to market yourself and your value. It enhances or detracts from your brand equity.

Communicating with power is one's ability to effectively deliver a message while conveying the essence of your brand through verbal and nonverbal cues. Job seekers who can succinctly articulate why they would be the best person for the job are likely to have an advantage over the competition.

To maximize your impact, you must carry yourself and interact in a manner that garners respect and that conveys confidence, competence, and credibility. Your job as an effective networker is to break through the clutter. To keep the focus where it belongs, control the communication, practice "your story" (see part I), and leverage your strategic networking tool kit.

The secret sauce for achieving break-through communication is NOT so secret. Sorry! In fact, it is akin to the keys for maintaining optimal health. Both require a personal commitment, focus, good habits and lots of practice in order to achieve and sustain peak performance. Another parallel for health and communication is that there are some variables you cannot fully control. In the case of health, your genetic makeup is something you are born with and therefore, you must find ways to work with what you have. The same is true for communication. Some people are gifted with great voices that seem to captivate others when they speak. While some elements are bestowed by nature, many are learned and honed through skill development and practice.

In the midst of an audience Q & A for a keynote presentation I gave, one of the attendees complimented me on my presentation style. To paraphrase, he said: "This is part commentary, part question. You have such as engaging presentation style. You are an excellent communicator. What is your secret?" After thanking him for the compliment, I went on to convey that my skills were developed and honed over many years. It certainly helped that I studied Marketing and Communications, but more importantly, I am a perpetual student. My natural tendency is introversion. Yes, that's correct. I am an introvert. Basically, an introvert is someone who gets energized and replenished by being alone and whose energy is drained by being around people. Psychology Today notes some of the common traits of introverts as:

- Very Self-aware
- Thoughtful
- Enjoys understanding details
- Interested in self-knowledge and self-understanding

- Tends to keep emotions private
- Quiet and reserved in large groups or around unfamiliar people

These traits are not necessarily ones you would expect from someone who is focused on networking. They are some traits that you might recognize when you think of some of the world's most famous introverts, past and present—Bill Gates, Abraham Lincoln, Christina Aguilera, Albert Einstein, Mahatma Gandhi, Rosa Parzks, Audrey Hepburn, Warren Buffett, Marissa Mayer and President Barack Obama.

As it relates to communication, some of the skills that are associated with excellent live communication – story telling, connecting with and openly engaging the audience, are those that can be acquired through practice. You don't have to do it alone. Use the positive, successful examples around you.

Enlist Allies and Ambassadors

Effective communicators know that some messages are best communicated by others. This is also true when it comes to promoting your brand. Activate your allies and your brand ambassadors to spread the word about you. You will need to adequately prepare them by spending the requisite time with them and keeping them up to date on your progress. ICCs in particular should be well versed about you. Similarly, you too can help to advance the agenda of your ICCs and MVCs, whose roles were described in part III.

Assume Positive Intent

When you assume positive motivations and exhibit uplifting behaviors, most people will respond in kind. If you are truly executing on your plan, you will make mistakes. Likewise, others in your network may not be as responsive as you think they should be. There are times when you will get stuck. As with anything else, a positive approach usually wins the day.

Confidence

Confidence in your communications delivery and in your strategic networking plan will come once you have done the hard work. As the saying goes, "It takes a lot of hard work to make things look easy." The effort that you put into your plan and, more importantly, into executing on your plan, helps you build confidence. That confidence can translate into opportunities that extend way beyond your grand vision.

Credibility

Establishing your credibility early in the process is important. Your potential ICCs in particular tend to have very short attention spans. They are very short on time, and most have little patience for sifting through whether or not you are worthy of their time. I know that to some, this may sound harsh. It's not personal. For those you seek to engage, do your homework, and send your bio in advance of the meeting—including your credentials. If they have an established relationship with someone who knows you well, have them put in a good word for you. It will go a long way toward paving the way for a successful interaction.

It is imperative that you assume nothing and find ways to let the key players know about your capabilities. You can weave this into conversations without being overly boastful or by placing your awards and diplomas in your office or business space. Ideally, you want the information to come from multiple sources, so the burden is not just on you in talking about yourself. Share key information, speaking engagements, and forums you are leading with your business associates. These things serve as a reminder that you are a player in the business community. Ultimately it is your responsibility to track and communicate your accomplishments.

Communicate with Impact—High-Impact Tips

Tip 1: Always approach your communications with a high degree of professionalism, and respect other people's time.

Tip 2: Use proper punctuation and capitalization in your professional e-mails. How you communicate online with your friends is your business; however, your communication in business and in the workplace is a reflection on you and your brand.

Tip 3: Seek opportunities to present and to speak, both at internal meetings and external forums. The discipline, skill, and oral communication used for presentations will serve you well and will raise your visibility.

Tip 4: Practice your speech or presentation. Please do not read your speech word for word. Ideally you should commit it to memory and use prompts or key phrases to jog your memory. If you are pressed for time or if memorization is not feasible due to the length or complexity of your speech, at least practice your prepared remarks out loud. Do this prior to giving your talk and build in pauses so that you are periodically looking at your audience.

Tip 5: Present and communicate with passion. If *you* are bored with the topic, why should others have to suffer through your presentation?

Tip 6: Prepare for meetings as you would a presentation, regardless of your role. If you are leading the meeting, take time to think through the role of the participants and their interests. Be clear about your objectives and those of your participants. Send an agenda in advance of the meeting. Respect the time of your colleagues and participants by starting and ending the meeting as scheduled.

Tip 7: Actively engage when you are a participant rather than the meeting leader. If you are playing the role of participant, read the agenda and think through your contribution to the meeting.

Tip 8: Listen. Listen. Listen intently, and ask thoughtful questions. This is another sign of engagement and respect.

Tip 9: Pay attention to your body language and your facial expressions. You want to convey interest, not boredom.

Tip 10: Follow through on your action items, and do what you said you would do.

Tip 11: Connect with your audience. You have an audience every day, whether it consists of coworkers, subordinates, other executives, or mentees. Put yourself in their shoes, and ask the basics—who, what, where, when, and how—relative to interpersonal connections.

Tip 12: Create an environment that makes others feel comfortable connecting with you. Identify ways in which you can deepen your business relationships. Put yourself in the other person's shoes and try a variety of approaches—invitations to events, hand-written notes, useful information and articles and the like. The notion of meaningful connection is incredibly important in the work environment and the marketplace.

Communication is a foundational pillar of your strategic networking plan. It is woven into the fabric of every interaction. Even the most seasoned professionals require an occasional refresher, so take this opportunity to identify areas where you can increase your effectiveness. Be sure to complete Making it Real.

Making It Real Action Exercise:
Increasing the Effectiveness of My Communications

Take Inventory and Take Action!

Now is the best time to start or to modify my approach to powerful communications. Make an assessment of my "how." The goal here is continuous improvement. Review the twelve communications tips from this chapter and identify the top three (or more) areas for improvement.

These are the actions I will take to improve the effectiveness of my communications:

1. _____
   _____
   _____
   _____
   _____
   _____

2. _____
   _____
   _____
   _____
   _____
   _____

3. _____
   _____
   _____
   _____
   _____
   _____

CHAPTER 14

NETWORKING ESSENTIALS AND ETIQUETTE

> *I've learned that people will forget what you said, people will forget what you did, but people will never forget how you made them feel.*
> —MAYA ANGELOU

In today's time-pressured, digital world, face-to-face communication remains a highly valued interaction. Treasure those moments to connect "live" whenever possible, and familiarize yourself with professional courtesies. Before you dismiss this chapter on etiquette as relevant only to young professionals, think again. Are there areas in which you are in need of a refresher? Fortunately, numerous books exist covering the soup to nuts of general etiquette. That is not the intent of this chapter. Here I will focus on some of the essentials for enhancing your networking effectiveness. I've developed an approach for networking engagement that is applicable for any relationship. I've dubbed this approach "HEARTS." It spells out the "how to" behaviors that are sometimes forgotten. In addition, I will cover some of the basics for business networking etiquette.

HEARTS—Networking Essentials

H—Honesty and integrity will help you build and maintain trusting productive relationships. Your actions should be consistent with your words.

People will pay close attention to what you do, not just what you say. Be transparent in your dealings, and do what you say you're going to do! Bring your authentic self to every interaction. If you don't, you will pay a tremendous price on your health, finances, and relationships.

E—Energy and enthusiasm are infectious twin attributes that you must exude. People want to associate with others who exhibit positive energy and are passionate about their work and their product(s). Show conviction in all aspects of your work, your communications, and your physical presence. While we're on *E*, let's not forget exercise. It does wonders for your mind, body, and energy level.

A—Attitude! Having a positive attitude and operating from a place of abundance accelerates growth. Abundant thinkers realize that there is enough for everyone and that by helping others and giving selflessly, *more* opportunities are created, not fewer. Give liberally and with a positive attitude.

R—"*R-E-S-P-E-C-T. Find out what it means to me.*" Thank you, Aretha Franklin, for calling attention to this important word. Respect is something that *everyone* wants, and this is true across all cultures. Demonstrate respect through your actions by valuing differences, adopting an inclusive approach, valuing the unique contributions of others, and communicating in culturally competent ways.

T—"Thanks" is a powerful six-letter word that cannot be overused. Be appreciative of the things that others do for you. Don't take them for granted. Never be too busy to say thank you. A simple handwritten card can differentiate you from the crowd and bring a smile to the receiver of your kind gesture. At a minimum, send a thank-you email.

S—Smile. Practice smiling. It's never too late to start. Make it part of your tool kit when you approach others and when you're on the phone. Unless the occasion is a sad one, this simple gesture makes you more approachable. It doesn't mean you have to grin from ear to ear. It's more about your approach, and smiling tends to break the ice.

Navigating the Networking Lunch

It is perfectly okay to extend invitations for lunch (or other meal) to people you are seeking to get to know better and with whom you have already established a relationship. E-mail is an acceptable method for a lunch invitation. It is generally a good idea to include multiple options for dates once your guest(s) have agreed to this method of connecting with you. Be clear about the purpose of the lunch. This will help to set the expectations for your meeting.

Punctuality is a must. Not only is punctuality expected, it reflects your level of professionalism and respect for the other person's time. Plan your day and travels accordingly so that you will arrive at the designated place at least five minutes ahead of schedule. In case of an emergency that causes you to be late, call ahead to the restaurant, and give your guests the courtesy of a message.

Prepare to have a conversation. Give some advance thought and planning for your networking connection. You don't need a script, but you should have a goal of what you hope to accomplish for the lunch meeting and key things you want to discuss.

As the one extending the invitation, you are expected to pay for the meal. Let your guest know that the lunch is your treat. You can articulate this verbally or immediately take the luncheon check when it arrives. Certainly, if your guest insists on paying for lunch or offers to go Dutch, it is okay to accept.

Lunch Table Tips (Selected Tips for the Business Luncheon)

1. Choose a lunch location that is convenient for your guest.
2. Request a telephone number that is frequently checked by your guest—ideally a business cell phone number. Provide your mobile contact information as well.
3. Once you arrive at the luncheon destination, put away your cell phone and any items that can cause distraction.

4. Give your guest a warm welcome and the best seating.
5. Place your napkin in your lap immediately after you are seated.
6. Allow your guest to order first.
7. Order foods that are easy to handle and that are less likely to end up on your clothing or between your teeth.
8. Use the appropriate utensils for your meal. When in doubt, use the utensils from the outside in.
9. Thank your wait staff and your guest(s).
10. Follow up your lunch meeting with a written communiqué. Yes, e-mail is fine, but a handwritten card is better, as it will make you stand out.

Returning Telephone Calls
Your network is broader than people you meet at business events; it also includes those in your day-to-day business dealings. When a work colleague calls, return the call as soon as possible—do not exceed forty-eight hours. Not returning the call of a colleague is disrespectful and rude, yet there seems to be an increasing acceptance of this unprofessional practice. *Do not* perpetuate this bad habit. It damages your brand and could later come back to haunt you.

If you are completely swamped, and the request can't be fulfilled immediately, at least acknowledge the contact, and let the person know that you plan to follow up later when your schedule eases.

Handling Other Networking Calls
Should you return telephone calls for those wishing to network with you? It depends. For those with whom you have an established connection, make a point of returning calls within forty-eight hours of contact. If you cannot meet this time frame, don't fret, but do acknowledge the call by either having your assistant get back to the person or call during off-peak hours.

If the call is specific, and you can take action, do so rather than pro-crastinate. For example, you met an executive who spoke at a conference you attended a few months ago. The person was very impressed by your presentation and called to invite you to present your topic at a business forum she is hosting. In this instance, if you have enough information to make an assessment, you can check your schedule, determine whether the opportunity makes sense for you, hold the time open, and schedule a spe-cific time to speak with the caller.

In another instance, you have received three calls from a hotshot entre-preneur you met at an event at which you spoke about the importance of networking. She is looking to meet with your marketing director and would like you to set up a meeting for her so she can do so. This is her third call to you within two business days. You did not give her your business card nor did you agree to any follow-up. Should you return the call? You are not obligated to do so, but it is up to you. You could let her know that your firm is already working with a vendor who offers the same services and is not in the market to make a change. Your assistant can place the call to her and ac-knowledge receipt of the message, letting her know that you will call at a later date, or you may choose to make time to have a brief conversation with her. In the priority scheme, she would not receive ICC or HVC priority.

Realistically, busy professionals cannot give equal weight to everyone who wishes to network with them. You have to be selective. In so doing, consider your networking tiers (ICC, HVC, and MVC) and align activi-ties with your goals. Above all, be respectful in your communications even when you say no.

When attending networking forums, schedule an hour within the two days following the session to return calls and to follow up on key connec-tions that you want to cultivate.

If you are following up on a discussion or commitment, it is okay to send more than one e-mail or telephone call to the person, as long as you are respectful. It's always wise to remind the person of where you met and about any agreed upon actions. Though well intentioned, people are often overwhelmed with e-mails and telephone calls. Be specific in your communications, and always be polite. When leaving a voice message, say your name, state your objective, and clearly provide the number where you can be reached. Repeat the number for your listener's convenience. It is annoying and inefficient to have to replay a message multiple times to try to decipher the person's name and/or telephone number. By leaving a detailed, succinct message, the receiver will have enough information to take action. Unless your topic is highly sensitive and confidential, don't leave them guessing regarding your call.

Social and Professional Networking Invitations

Should you accept invitations from social networking and professional networking websites? Again, it depends. Be careful whom you befriend and invite into your personal network. I recommend reserving personal networks such as Facebook (not Facebook Pages) for friends and family. Do not accept invitations from those wishing to befriend you in this way if the person is not a personal friend. For professional networks, it is not as clear-cut. For professional invitations, such as those on LinkedIn, you should determine your objective and your plans for using the tool and let that be your guide. If you are looking to build the largest set of professional connections possible, then you should accept all requests. On the other hand, if you are looking to use the tool selectively for endorsements and referrals of trusted sources with whom you have close connection (e.g., your HVCs), then you should accept invitations only from those of whom you have a professional working knowledge.

A Word about Invitations to Paid Events

If you are inviting someone to a paid event, please be honest and up-front about it. Do not use the word "guest" as in "please come as my guest" unless you plan to pick up the tab or provide complimentary tickets. I've received such an invitation on a number of occasions. After accepting, I got a second message letting me know that the cost of the event was $250 and that I needed to forward a check for that amount to the individual. In one instance, I paid the fee even though I felt bamboozled. I was not amused by the sly approach they used. This method of operating is a major violation of the first of the HEARTS approach—honesty. Be up-front about invitations that require an outlay of cash. What do you think I did when I received the next invitation from that individual asking me to come as their guest? 'Nuff said.

Company Dinners or Community Galas

You may work for a large organization, may have purchased a ticket to support a community event, or perhaps are a guest of an organization hosting a dinner. Regardless of how you got there, these events are great opportunities for networking. While it is certainly an opportunity to see some people you may know, make a point of connecting with at least two people you do not know. Always introduce yourself to the other guests or colleagues at the table. If you are the table host, be sure to greet each person at your table, even if you already know them. This simple gesture will make your tablemates feel welcome.

Referrals

If you know the person well and can personally vouch for him or her, by all means do so. When you do refer someone, whenever possible, make a warm, in-person introduction. Depending on the nature of the referral, you can schedule breakfast or lunch with the parties. This works well for important referrals that can likely lead to significant business opportunities or win/win alliances. If this is not feasible, provide some context for the referral. You can do this by e-mail or by voice mail.

Be considerate of other people's time when referring others. In today's hectic business environment, time is very precious. Before referring others, be thoughtful, and use those requests judiciously.

Job References

For professional-level jobs, recruiters will often leverage their networks to find out about candidates. Likewise, job seekers will reach out to their networks to find out about a company, the hiring executive, or the opportunity. When using someone as a reference, make sure you let the person know in advance and obtain permission to do so. Sometimes those who have been in the workforce for an extended length of time forget these career basics. You should always arm your reference with a recent copy of your resume, a description of the job for which you are being considered, and key points that you think are relevant to communicate.

Business Card Exchange

As I mentioned previously, your business card is a marketing and networking tool. Make sure that it is high quality and professionally designed. Use a business card case to ensure easy access to your cards and to protect them from discoloration, stains, and the like.

In keeping with our strategic networking approach, distribute your card selectively. First, establish some common ground or mutual interest. You should have a reason and agreement when exchanging business cards.

How to make the exchange:

- When giving your business card, hold the card at the corner with the information facing toward the other person.
- When receiving someone else's card, take a second to look at the card and thank them.
- Use the back of the card to jot a note to yourself about the person or any action items relevant to your discussion. You may also want to include tidbits to help you remember the person, for example, "Simmons grad, red suit, knows Pam." I find this to be particularly useful at large events where you may end the evening with five or more cards.

- As I mentioned previously, I recommend that you use CardCam or a similar app to transfer cards to your contact system. After the meeting or event, follow up on any action items that you have noted on the card, and transfer the card to your contact system. While you're at it, you should send a LinkedIn request to your new contact.

Name Tags

Wear your name tag on your right-hand side. This makes it a lot easier to glance at the name tag when shaking hands. If you are hosting the event, be sure to place both the first name and last name on the name tag, and use a large, easy-to-read font.

Make Them the Center of Your Universe

You're at a reception having a wonderful time getting to know Sue. There's just one annoying problem: Sue keeps glancing around the room. The minute she sees Joe, she abruptly ends the conversation and greets him. There are legitimate reasons why this could happen. It is possible that Sue invited Joe and wants to make sure he is welcomed appropriately. However, you are feeling dumped by Sue, right? Managing transitions can be tricky. In this instance, the appropriate thing for Sue to do is to give you a heads-up. "Jenny, just so you know, I'm not being rude—I am expecting my colleague Joe to arrive any minute. He's on a tight schedule, so once he arrives, I need to introduce him to Jan, so forgive me if it seems that I keep glancing toward the door." Better still, Sue should wait for Joe near the entrance to avoid this scenario altogether. Make your networking colleague the center of your attention.

Handling RSVPs

Give your requester the courtesy of a response. The abbreviation RSVP used on most invitations is short for the French term *Respondez s'il vous plait*. It means "respond if you please" or simply "please respond." Whether your invitation arrives in writing or in an electronic communiqué such as Evite or e-mail, you should let your requester know your intentions. This common courtesy allows your host to plan accordingly and is appropriate not just for formal events but for meetings as well.

Etiquette and Your Brand

How you interact with people and the attributes you exhibit in doing so make a marked difference in how you are perceived and positively impacts the lives of others. Commit yourself to embracing the HEARTS networking essentials and to practicing good business etiquette.

CHAPTER 15

REFLECTIONS

As I reflect on my early life in Barbados, West Indies, my mother's words echo in my ears. While she did not have a formal education, she had a master's degree in emotional intelligence and a doctorate in faith. She would say things like, "We may be poor financially, but we're not poor in spirit. In all your getting, get an education. Hold your head up high. Take pride in how you carry yourself. Dream big; don't let what you see around you define you. I expect the best from you." These powerful words required a huge leap of faith considering we lived in a two-room shack without running water or electricity. Yet her faith was supported by action.

As I look back on the life of my now-deceased mother, I realize she was a consummate networker. She gravitated toward positive people who were doing great things. She was genuinely supportive in helping others advance, even when she did not yet see a way out for herself. She was true to her word and did not let her circumstances define her. As a result, she raised three well-educated daughters, all of whom are carrying the torch to help others improve their lives.

How many times have you heard the sayings "Have a dream," "Live your passion," and "Do what you love"? Easier said than done, right? Sometimes life looks so easy for the people who have "made it." It's as if they had a roadmap and followed it straight to their dreamland. In reality, success is built one relationship at a time, and I would add that success is built one confession at a time. My mother was a great example that what we believe and what we speak can become powerful truths when we take positive action. Her faith led her to seek out like-minded people, many of whom helped her to achieve success in life and to create a legacy for her children.

Because of the fulfillment of her dream, I am living my dream. CEO, author, speaker—who knew? Deep down inside, I knew. It was the deconstruction of the journey that shed light on the principles that I've shared with you. I hope that you will let this be the beginning of yet another grand vision. I wish you success on your journey, and I look forward to connecting with you.

God bless,
Juliette C. Mayers
CEO, Inspiration Zone LLC
@jcmayers
juliette@juliettemayers.com
www.juliettemayers.com
www.inspirationzoneLLC.com
www.LinkedIn/in/juliettemayers

REFERENCES

Canfield, Jack, Mark Victor Hansen, and Les Hewitt. *The Power of Focus*. Florida: HCI, 2000.

Joel Comm, *Twitter Power, Hoboken, New Jersey, 2010*

Fields, Martha R.A. *Love Your Work By Loving Your Life*. Cambridge, Massachusetts: Marmerv, 2004.

Giang, Vivian, The Surprising Ways that Networking Fails Women. *Fast Company Magazine*, March 11, 2015

Heard, Marian Langston. *The Complete Leader: Your Path to the Top: Tried and True Principles, Good Habits, and Advice to Help You Lead*. Natick, Massachusetts: Heard Enterprises, 2004.

Jordan, Vernon E., and Annette Gordon-Reed. *Vernon Can Read! A Memoir*. New York: Basic Civitas, 2003.
Latifah, Queen, and Karen Hunter. *Ladies First: Revelations of a Strong Woman*. New York: William Morrow, 1999.
Mayers, Juliette, *A Black Woman's Guide to Networking*, North Charleston, SC, CreateSpace, 2011

Misner, Ivan R., David G. Alexander, and Brian Hilliard. *Networking like a Pro: Turning Contacts into Connections*. Irvine, California: Entrepreneur, 2009.

Rutledge, Patricia Anne. *Sams Teach Yourself LinkedIn*, Indianapolis, Indiana, Sams/Pearson, 2011.

Schawbel, Dan. *Me 2.0: 4 Steps to Building Your Future*. New York: Kaplan Pub., 2010.

Scott, David Meerman. *The New Rules of Marketing and PR: How to Use Social Media, Blogs, News Releases, Online Video, & Viral Marketing to Reach Buyers Directly*. Hoboken, New Jersey: John Wiley & Sons, 2010.

Shih, Clara Chung-wai. *The Facebook Era: Tapping Online Social Networks to Market, Sell, and Innovate*. Upper Saddle River, New Jersey: Prentice Hall, 2011.

Net Working Master Class (NMC)

Excerpts from a 2011 interview with esteemed executives who are adept at networking have been included for reference. Some content has been updated for this publication. NMCs who's comments are featured in The Guide to Strategic Networking are:

Josefina Bonilla, President and CEO, Josefina Bonilla, CEO and Chief Marketing Officer of Color Media Group, LLC

Martha R. A. Fields, CEO, Fields Associates

Stacy Blake-Beard, PhD, Professor of Management and Faculty Affiliate, Center for Gender in Organizations

Cheryl Ginyard-Jones

Helen Drinan, President and CEO, Simmons College

Paul Guzzi, Chairman, Citi Center for the Performing Arts

Marian L. Heard, president and CEO, Oxen Hill Partners; retired president and CEO, the United Way of Massachusetts Bay; CEO of the United Way of New England

J. Keith Motley, PhD, Chancellor, University of Massachusetts Boston

Colette A. M. Phillips, president and CEO, CPC Global and founder of Get Konnected)

Linda Watters, vice president, government relations, John Hancock

ACKNOWLEDGMENTS

I am grateful for the love and support of my wonderful husband and partner of 24 years, Darryl Mayers. As always, you are the wind beneath my wings and I cherish and appreciate you. Thanks for your edits and your feedback on this second book. Danielle, thanks for your patience with me as I juggled the numerous balls in our daily lives. It's hard to believe that you will be off to college shortly. I love and appreciate you. D'Anna, thank you for your encouragement. I look forward to your frequent calls; particularly the ones that are "just because," – how blessed am I? Thank you. I love and appreciate you.

I am thankful for the support of my dear friend Martha who was the source of my inspiration for the writing of this second book. I am blessed to have you in my life. Thank you for all that you do and for being such a great friend. My professional circle is deep and wide, as is my support circle. I'd like to thank everyone who offered a word of encouragement. Happy tenth anniversary to my ELC Pipeline Sisters, Crystal Ashby, Joy Booker, Karen Boothe Begley, Stephanie Browne, Cheryl Ginyard-Jones, Toni Leatherberry, Andrea Scipio, Tracey Gray Walker and Pat Washington. It's hard to believe that ten years has flown by. Your support and sisterhood means the world to me. I also want to congratulate my sisters in the Middlesex Chapter of the Links Incorporated and president, Paula Wright on forty years of friendship and service. You are each phenomenal women and I am proud to have you in my circle. To the Partnership's Next Generation Executive class of 2015, you rock! Carol, thanks for your leadership and support. A special shout-out to my SBA CEO cohort, Beth Davis and Bob Nelson.

To my executive mentors, friends and advisors some of whom have provided quotes for this book. I am thrilled to be a part of your village. Special thanks to:

Maureen Alphonse-Charles
Susan Archer
Phyllis Barajas
Jeff Bellows
Stacy Blake-Beard
Josefina Bonilla
Ron and Betty Crutcher
Michael Curry
Helen Drinan
Martha R.A. Fields
Carol Fulp
Janine Fondon
Yvonne Garcia
Carolyn Golden Hebsgaard
Maxcene Latin
Paul Guzzi
Beverly Edgehill
Marian Heard
Elvoid Mayers
J. Keith Motley
Claire Muhm
Phil Johnston
Colette Phillips
Paula Price
Bob Rivers

Dorothy Terrell
Alberto Vasallo
Linda Watters
Bennie Wiley
Darnell Williams
Frederica Williams
Sabrina Williams

ABOUT THE AUTHOR

A well-rounded business executive and networking expert, Juliette Mayers delivers measurable results for organizations, communities, and individuals.

Mayers is president and CEO of Inspiration Zone LLC (IZL), a firm specializing in multicultural consulting, brand management, and thought leadership. Mayers has successfully integrated traditional business strategy, multicultural expertise and insights to provide value-driven solutions that position brands for success in the global marketplace. Her breadth of experience spans three key industries: financial services, communications, and health care. She has held senior leadership roles in strategy, marketing, diversity, planning, and board leadership at Fortune 500 and large not-for-profit organizations.

As principal of Inspiration Zone, she acts as principal consultant to organizations and individuals to identify opportunities for increasing revenue and driving engagement. Prior to launching IZL, Mayers was a marketing executive at Blue Cross Blue Shield MA(BCBSMA) where she led multicultural marketing and spearheaded the company's strategy and employer programs to address racial and ethnic disparities in health care. Mayers also created and led Blue Cross Blue Shield's award-winning Multicultural Ambassadors program, an engagement and business initiative with over 90% percent engagement scores annually.

A passionate leader, Mayers serves on the boards of Eastern Bank, the US. Small Business Federal Advisory Board, the Massachusetts Workforce Investment Board, and The Boston Club. She is emeritus board president of Action for Boston Community Development (ABCD), a $150 million antipoverty organization and the largest community-action agency in the country.

Throughout her stellar career, Mayers has amassed a body of work that has received national acclaim. Recent awards include the Boston Business Journal's Leadership Award for Multicultural Marketing, the Hispanic-American Chamber's Small Business Champion award, *Profiles in Diversity Journal's Women Worth Watching* award, the Sojourner Truth Business Leadership Award, and the Girl Scouts of Eastern MA Leading Women's Award.

Mayers is the author of *A Black Woman's Guide to Networking* which was featured in a variety of media outlets, including WHDH, WCVB-TV, CBS, the *Boston Globe, Harlem World,* and *Exhale Magazine.* She is a sought-after speaker on a variety of leadership and networking topics.

Mayers is an alumna of Simmons Graduate School of Management, where she earned her MBA, and Northeastern University, where she received her BS in marketing.

www.inspirationzoneLLC.com
www.juliettemayers.com

Made in the USA
Middletown, DE
03 June 2016